THE STATE OF (IN)VISIBLE BLACK EUROPE: RACE, RIGHTS & POLITICS

HEARING

BEFORE THE

COMMISSION ON SECURITY AND COOPERATION IN EUROPE

ONE HUNDRED TENTH CONGRESS

SECOND SESSION

APRIL 29, 2008

Printed for the use of the
Commission on Security and Cooperation in Europe

[CSCE 110–2–10]

Available via http://www.csce.gov

U.S. GOVERNMENT PRINTING OFFICE

63–749 PDF   WASHINGTON : 2012

For sale by the Superintendent of Documents, U.S. Government Printing Office
Internet: bookstore.gpo.gov   Phone: toll free (866) 512–1800; DC area (202) 512–1800
Fax: (202) 512–2250   Mail: Stop SSOP, Washington, DC 20402–0001

COMMISSION ON SECURITY AND COOPERATION IN EUROPE

LEGISLATIVE BRANCH COMMISSIONERS

<table>
<tr><td align="center">HOUSE</td><td align="center">SENATE</td></tr>
<tr><td>

ALCEE L. HASTINGS, Florida,
Chairman
LOUISE McINTOSH SLAUGHTER,
New York
MIKE McINTYRE, North Carolina
HILDA L. SOLIS, California
G.K. BUTTERFIELD, North Carolina
CHRISTOPHER H. SMITH, New Jersey
ROBERT B. ADERHOLT, Alabama
JOSEPH R. PITTS, Pennsylvania
MIKE PENCE, Indiana

</td><td>

BENJAMIN L. CARDIN, Maryland,
Co-Chairman
RUSSELL D. FEINGOLD, Wisconsin
CHRISTOPHER J. DODD, Connecticut
HILLARY RODHAM CLINTON, New York
JOHN F. KERRY, Massachusetts
SAM BROWNBACK, Kansas
GORDON SMITH, Oregon
SAXBY CHAMBLISS, Georgia
RICHARD BURR, North Carolina

</td></tr>
</table>

EXECUTIVE BRANCH COMMISSIONERS

David J. Kramer, Department of State
VACANT, Department of Defense
David Bohigian, Department of Commerce

(II)

THE STATE OF (IN)VISIBLE BLACK EUROPE: RACE, RIGHTS & POLITICS

APRIL 29, 2008

COMMISSIONERS

Page

Hon. Alcee L. Hastings, Chairman, Commission on Security and Cooperation in Europe 1
Hon. David J. Kramer, Executive Branch Commissioner, Assistant Secretary of State for Democracy, Human Rights and Labor 3
Hon. G.K. Butterfield, Commissioner, Commission on Security and Cooperation in Europe 6
Hon. Christopher H. Smith, Ranking Member, Commission on Security and Cooperation in Europe 16

MEMBERS

Hon. Barbara Lee (D–9) a Member of Congress from the State of California 6
Hon. Carolyn C. Kilpatrick (D–13) a Member of Congress from the State of Michigan 15
Hon. Donald M. Payne (D–10) a Member of Congress from the State of New Jersey 32

WITNESSES

Joe Frans, Vice Chair, United Nations Working Group on People of African Descent, and former Swedish Parliamentarian 3
Gary Younge, British Columnist, The Guardian Newspaper .. 7
Philomena Essed, Antioch University, the Netherlands, Equal Treatment Commission 16
Allison Blakely, Author and Historian, Boston University 19
Clarence Lusane, International Race Politics Author, American University 22

APPENDICES

Prepared statement of Hon. Alcee L. Hastings 39
Prepared statement of Hon. Benjamin L. Cardin, Co-Chairman, Commission on Security and Cooperation in Europe . 41

IV

	Page
Prepared statement of Hon. G.K. Butterfield	43
Prepared statement of Joe Frans	44
Prepared statement of Gary Younge	46
Prepared statement of Philomena Essed	48
Prepared statement of Allison Blakely	56
Prepared statement of Clarence Lusane	59
Prepared statement submitted for the record by Boris Kodjoe, Actor	61
Material submitted for the record by:	
Brima Conteh, DIASPORA AFRIQUE	62
Initiative Black Germans (ISD)	68
Black European Women Congress	71

THE STATE OF (IN)VISIBLE BLACK EUROPE: RACE, RIGHTS & POLITICS

April 29, 2008

COMMISSION ON SECURITY AND COOPERATION IN EUROPE

WASHINGTON, DC

The hearing was held at 9:58 a.m. in room B–318, Rayburn House Office Building, Washington, DC, Hon. Alcee L. Hastings, Chairman, Commission on Security and Cooperation in Europe, presiding.

Commissioners present: Hon. Alcee L. Hastings, Chairman, Commission on Security and Cooperation in Europe; Hon. G.K. Butterfield, Commissioner, Commission on Security and Cooperation in Europe; and Hon. David J. Kramer, Executive Branch Commissioner, Department of State.

Members present: Hon. Barbara Lee (D–9) a Member of Congress from the State of California; Hon. Carolyn C. Kilpatrick (D–13) a Member of Congress from the State of Michigan; and Hon. Donald M. Payne (D–10) a Member of Congress from the State of New Jersey.

Witnesses present: Joe Frans, Vice Chair, United Nations Working Group on People of African Descent, and former Swedish Parliamentarian; Gary Younge, British columnist, The Guardian Newspaper; Allison Blakely, Author and Historian, Boston University; Philomena Essed, Antioch University, the Netherlands, Equal Treatment Commission; and Clarence Lusane, International Race Politics Author, American University.

HON. ALCEE L. HASTINGS, CHAIRMAN, COMMISSION ON SECURITY AND COOPERATION IN EUROPE

Mr. HASTINGS. Good morning. Let me call the hearing to order.

Ladies and gentlemen, thank you for your answers in this morning hearing focused on the experience of Blacks in Europe.

For many years I've traveled through Europe as a tourist, Member of Congress, President of the OSCE Parliamentary Assembly, and now as Chairman of the Helsinki Commission. On those trips I'd also meet other Black people living or traveling in Europe, who were thrilled to meet another Black person.

This was especially true when I was traveling in the former Soviet Union. Not always so thrilling were the stories they would share with me of the racism they faced.

And worse, I, too, was the victim of racial profiling by authorities and blatant discrimination, such as when I was refused service in several establishments in different places in Europe. My memory serves me several times at the Frankfurt Airport, in Madrid, and in other places that one would not normally expect that to occur.

In this regard there are a number of similarities between my experiences as a Black American and those of Black Europeans. So one central goal of this hearing is to highlight and address the very real problems of racism and discrimination faced by Black Europeans.

Another goal is also to recall the contributions Blacks have made to Europe and the world by removing the cloak of invisibility that for so long has shown as a shroud.

Recognizing and d-mythologizing the roles of Blacks in European history and modern day society has become a necessity, given the rise of virulent anti-immigrant campaigns that target non-Whites in the aftermath of 9/11 and the London bombings. Whether Blacks were forced or chose to assist in Europe's development, they did play a role that should be noted.

As globalization continues to bring the world closer together, how European countries choose to define themselves and their peoples affects all of us and will most certainly affect how I am viewed, as well as others, and treated within Europe's borders.

The third goal of this hearing is to then develop partnerships with those overseas committed to addressing these problems. Too often we highlight the problems within countries without noting the efforts that are being made, be they government, civil society or even the private sector.

The OSCE High Commissioner on National Minorities, as well as the EU Fundamental Rights Agency, has compiled reports on European countries' positive initiatives, ranging from affirmative action to housing and education and desegregation.

These are all efforts that have already been tried in the United States, and we need to be asking ourselves how we can best extend a helping hand so that Europeans don't repeat some of the mistakes we made here in developing and implementing these programs.

The fourth point, which requires us to be honest with ourselves, is that there are a number of very real barriers to addressing inclusion goals for Black Europeans, ranging from the small size of some communities to a need for differences in approach for recent migrant versus more established communities.

I'm glad to have such esteemed witnesses here today to present thoughts on all these issues and I'd like to introduce Mr. Joe Frans from Sweden and Mr. Gary Younge joining us from the U.K. via New York to speak about their work.

Unfortunately, due to scheduling constraints around Mr. Kodjoe's schedule—he's in the Broadway play, "Cat on a Hot Tin Roof"—he's been unable to be here today. He has, however, indicated his support for this and future initiatives on Blacks in Europe and asked that I enter his statement in the record, which I will.

I would also at this time like to enter the statements of some of our European friends, the Initiative of Black Germans, the Diaspora Afrique, and the Black European Women's Congress.

We've been joined by Assistant Secretary of State, my colleague and Commissioner, David Kramer, who is the Assistant Secretary of State for Democracy, Human Rights and Labor and Commissioner Kramer, I give you the floor.

HON. DAVID J. KRAMER, EXECUTIVE BRANCH COMMISSIONER, ASSISTANT SECRETARY OF STATE FOR DEMOCRACY, HUMAN RIGHTS AND LABOR

Sec. KRAMER. Mr. Chairman, thank you very much. It's good to be with you this morning. Thank you very much for convening this hearing this morning on a very important subject and I very much look forward to hearing the witnesses. I appreciate your opening comments, and I think without further ado, I turn it over back to you.

Mr. HASTINGS. We will start, then, with Joe Frans, who is the Vice Chair of the United Nations Working Group on People of African Descent and a former Swedish parliamentarian.

Mr. Frans, I didn't have much time this morning, but I imagine you know Göran Lennmarker, who was my immediate successor in the Parliamentary Assembly and he will be followed by Gary Younge, who is a British columnist at the Guardian Newspaper and their resumes are on the table outside, so I won't go into all of their curriculum vitae.

So, Mr. Frans, if I could start with you, please, sir? And then we will have our second panel come up.

JOE FRANS, VICE CHAIR, UNITED NATIONS WORKING GROUP ON PEOPLE OF AFRICAN DESCENT, AND FORMER SWEDISH PARLIAMENTARIAN

Dr. FRANS. Thank you, Chairman Hastings, Commissioner Kramer, ladies and gentlemen. It is indeed a great pleasure and honor to be with you here today, and I'm very, very pleased that you have chosen the topic of African diaspora of Blacks in Europe for this particular hearing.

It is a timely intervention and a most relevant one. This is simply because Europe is currently undergoing a soul searching experience of its own and I think this dialogue can contribute to that.

A few weeks ago a good friend of mine from Sweden, the mayor of Sodertalje, was here to witness, and I'd like to say that I endorse every bit of what he said and also I am very thankful that the Chair raised the issue on the floor of he House, which I wish to thank you for.

I'd like to begin this brief presentation by paying tribute to the millions of African people abducted and enslaved and to those who sacrificed their lives in fighting for national liberation in Africa and in the diaspora. They have inspired us, and they have inspired our thinking and indeed generated our current desire to contribute as a diaspora to the development of Africa and to the people of humanity as a whole.

The African diaspora consists of people of African origin living outside the continent, irrespective of their citizenship and nationality, and who are willing to contribute to the development of the continent of Africa and the building of Africans.

Today there are over 3.3 million people of African descent living in Europe. This is according to the Eurostat, but we know that it is much more than that.

Mr. HASTINGS. Could you repeat the figure again for me? I'm sorry. I was distracted.

Dr. FRANS. This is the figure from the Eurostat. It states that 3.3 million people of African descendant, out of which, I should say, over about a million come from south Sahara in Africa.

In the post-World War II area, the need for cheap labor to re-build Europe resulted in the influx of Africans to Europe. The post-independence era further generated an inflow of African students, and political conflicts in Africa itself, the cold war and the related global competition for economic development have also generated an inflow of asylum seekers and refugees and in addition, there has been a steady stream of African-European families who have chosen to settle in Europe as a matter of choice.

Today, beside the above reasons, the benefits of the trickle of migrants are double-sided. On the one hand, the reserve of cheap labor, often described as unwanted, is viewed by the regulator as being in the flow of migrants across the Mediterranean in scanty boats and with life itself at stake and literally swimming the last mile.

On the other hand, the question of whether attracting and sourcing highly skilled migrants from Africa to Europe are needed to sustain gains for Africa must be weighed. Basically, African countries are funding the education of their nationals, only to see them contributing to other countries' growth and development, with seemingly little or no return on their investment.

Yet at closer look, Africans are contributing to the development of Europe's identity and European identity and of the African continent itself. Some estimate that the Africans working abroad send home some $45 billion a year. That's bigger than the total development aid and also bigger than the total current direct investment in Africa.

What we need to do is to galvanize this amount into something that one could term as diaspora direct investment to make it more visible and to use it in the development of Africa.

However, the challenges of integrating the new work force in Europe itself remain. After the concluding session of the European Congress at [inaudible] in 2002, a political declaration was adopted by the Ministers of the Council of Europe member states, and in that document the government concluded that the continued and violent occurrence of racism is an issue of concern and that challenges of integrating young people, immigrants and other groups remain, especially in the labor market, where discrimination is present.

A report presented by the British Trade Union Congress had views that at every level of working life, many Black workers are being denied training opportunities, despite often being better qualified than their counterparts.

Discriminatory practices at work are still preventing too many workers in Europe of African descent from fulfilling their potential. However, statistics in the public domain to support arguments of violence and discrimination in the workplace in Europe are embarrassingly lacking. Without official statistics, effective responses cannot be devised.

One of the most common indicators of labor market inequality is the rate of unemployment of former immigrants and minorities. In 2005, it was reported that the unemployment rates for such groups were all significantly higher than for the majority population in many European countries.

It is quite clear that there are thousands of Africans, people of African descent, living in miserable conditions in Europe. Those without legal documents have no access to the welfare state, are exploited as cheap labor, and have no human rights at all.

Quite clearly, then, racism and discrimination are relevant to understanding the commonality of challenges of people of African descent in Europe.

The most important sectors, I believe, which we need to address in coming to terms with the everyday racism, but also structured racism and discrimination, still remain within the sectors of housing, of education, in the criminal justice system and in the health sector.

Yet, Mr. Chairman, let me say that there are also positive stories to tell about the integration of Blacks in Europe. There are also success stories to talk about. All countries have constitutional frameworks against discrimination, and there are institutional organizations like the Ombudsmen and other institutions in Europe that work and are working actively to combat racism and discrimination.

There are many successful legal stories in politics and policy dialogue in business and education.

Yet I have chosen to focus my brief presentation on those issues that demand our attention in framing policy—those issues that need solutions, those issues that need debate, and those issues that will define our future in defending the integrity of the human creation as such.

Those issues are integration, migration, discrimination as such, and development as a whole in shaping the new European identity. I think we cannot but have to deal with these issues in those sectors that I have mentioned; otherwise, we will come to a situation where the society will come into conflict with itself.

Mr. Chairman, one policy idea that could benefit from your support is the promotion of what I call the transatlantic dialogue on the experiences of African descent.

I think Black Europe could benefit from that kind of dialogue on how our brothers and sisters here in the United States have done and share the experiences and together help to create and formulate new ideas and help structure a new European identity.

I would welcome both your support and assistance in making this happen. Thank you.

Mr. HASTINGS. I'm very pleased to have been joined by my good friend and colleague from California, Congresswoman Barbara Lee. Congresswoman Lee is not a member of the Helsinki Commission, but she is a distinguished internationalist serving on several committees, including the Foreign Affairs Committee, and has had substantial involvement in the issue at hand.

If you have anything that you'd like to say at this time, Congresswoman Lee, you're welcome to do so.

HON. BARBARA LEE (D–9) A MEMBER OF CONGRESS FROM THE STATE OF CALIFORNIA

Ms. LEE. Well, Congressman Hastings, let me first thank you very much for your leadership and your vision and your insight, which led to putting this forum together today.

For me personally this is so important. I had the privilege to live in England in 1964 and 1965. In fact, my oldest son was born in London and it was during that period that I met, of course, Africans in the diaspora, people from the West Indies, from all over, the continent, and especially from Africa.

It was glaring that we face many of the same problems as African Americans here and I often thought wouldn't it be powerful if people of African descent came together to seek solutions to our common problems, to address what the realities are, based on what our witnesses are talking about, and come together to really turn the big issues that we're addressing into real opportunities? And the power of that would be very awesome.

So thank you very much. This is a moment to behold.

I want to welcome our witnesses and thank all of you for being here. I came back from California late last night so I could be here for an hour or so before I move on, and I really appreciate that.

Mr. HASTINGS. I thank you so much. When we planned this hearing, we thought we would be in session, and obviously members have to make adjustments accordingly, and I appreciate you having done so.

Ms. LEE. This is so important.

Mr. HASTINGS. We have also been joined by Commissioner G.K. Butterfield, my good friend from North Carolina.

G.K., we've just heard from one witness, but in light of the fact G.K. is a Helsinki Commissioner and also a well traveled individual that I've had the good fortune of traveling with abroad on numerous occasions, if you have any opening comments, we would welcome them.

HON. G.K. BUTTERFIELD, COMMISSIONER, COMMISSION ON SECURITY AND COOPERATION IN EUROPE

Mr. BUTTERFIELD. I don't have very many, Mr. Chairman. Let me just thank you for convening this hearing today. Like Congresswoman Barbara Lee, I came back this morning as well for this hearing. I looked forward to this day all week. I did not realize that we would not be in session today, but we made the effort, and we are here, despite the fact that we had a United States Senator in my district last night.

Mr. HASTINGS. Who would that be? [Laughter.]

Mr. BUTTERFIELD. We were with him until about midnight. So thank you very much for the hearing, and I look forward to the remaining witness.

Mr. HASTINGS. Thank you very much.

Congresswoman Lee, you spoke of my vision and insight and you know me—about people that work with us in these offices, actually I'd like to credit just for the record Dr. Mischa Thompson, who really has been our brain trust in this matter and I did not know that one of our persons that works with us—just recently in Vienna posted there—is Winsome Packer and I looked out and just happened to see her out there. Winsome also has been helping the entire Helsinki staff.

Dr. Younge? I haven't gotten away from you yet, so please, sir.

GARY YOUNGE, BRITISH COLUMNIST, THE GUARDIAN NEWSPAPER

Dr. YOUNGE. Chairman Hastings, distinguished members of the Commission, thank you very much for inviting me and convening this meeting.

I want to start with a personal story, which is about my mother, who came from London from Barbados in the early 60s with a British passport and two A levels in European history and English literature. She could quote from "A Winter's Tale," but you seek a hurricane.

Before she left the islands, she was given orientation classes to prepare for her life in Britain and they told her to wear flannel pajamas and a woolen hat, but they said nothing about people shouting abuse at her in the street.

My mother came of her own free will, but she also came because she was asked by the British Government, who paid her way and she was asked to build one of the nation's most cherished institutions, the National Health Service. Racism and cold aside, two of the things that would strike her when she arrived were that most British people seem to know very little about their own country and even less about the nations their country had occupied.

In the words of Gilbert, a Jamaican immigrant in Andrea Levy's award-winning novel "Small Island," "I had just one question. Let me ask the mother country just this one simple question, 'How come England did not know me?'"

Well, these elements of my mother's stories are going to form the basis of my testimony today, because they draw on some of the central threads of the Black European experience as it stands in difference and similarity to the American Black experience.

Europe did have a civil rights movement, and it took place at roughly the same time as the American civil rights movement, and around the same issues, by and large—the right to vote, opposition to segregation and a more equal share of resources.

It did not take place in Europe. For the most part, it primarily took place abroad in Algeria, Ghana, India, Mozambique, Congo, and so on. That's left the local White indigenous population in Europe with little understanding of a sense of historical responsibility to those whom it once colonized.

The screams of the oppressed tortured by colonialism were actually continents away and neither heard nor heeded at home. So it's been little in the way of moral reckoning with our past and when it comes to domestic matters, there is little in the way of historical literacy that would explain either European power or the presence of non-White people in Europe.

In the words of the venerable Director of the Institute of Race Relations in Britain, Ambalavaner Sivanandan, "We are here because you were there. If you didn't know you were there, how could you understand why we are here?"

Ignorance can and has led to severe racial antagonism, which over the past 20 years has reinstalled itself as a permanent fixture in European political culture. Fascism, or at least a xenophile-based racist and nationalist trait that [inaudible] allow manifestation, has returned as a mainstream ideology in Europe.

Its advocates not only run in elections, but win them. They control local councils and sit in parliament. In Austria, Belgium, Denmark, France, and Italy, hard right nationalist and anti-immigrant policies regularly receive more than 10 percent of the vote. In Norway, it's 22 percent; in Sweden, 29.

In Austria, the Right wing are in government; in Switzerland, the anti-immigrant Swiss People's Party, which is the largest party, is still in government, and after recent elections, they're about to return to government again.

Now, a central point of these parties' platforms rests on the notion that each European nation is its own mono-racial and mono-cultural unit into which non-White people have only recent come and must on entry either conform or be banished.

This, of course, is hinged on an entirely mythical notion of wide European uniformity, historical illiteracy about the length of time that non-White people have been in Europe, and a mistaken desire to defend Europeanness against the uncivilized and the unwashed.

Conversely to this trend on a daily level of cultural interaction, it is actually difficult to imagine a continent without non-White people. In literature, music and sport particularly, we have become so inextricably intertwined into the national fabric that to unpick us would make the whole cloth unravel.

In Britain rates of racial intermarriage are high. One in two Caribbean men and one in three Caribbean women have relationships with White people. Political culture and popular culture are in dislocation and moving in contradictory directions.

It's difficult to imagine Europe with non-White people, but that has not stopped many from trying. Particularly since September 11th, the push to assimilate some into a society that one has to educate, employ or respect them has become particularly intense.

Like many, my mother, who took a low-paid, steady job, the industries that non-White people came into depended largely on the countries they went to and came from, but they took the jobs that the local people did not want and the industries and sectors our parents went into have for the most part, shrunk or been decimated, leaving relatively little opportunities for their children.

In Europe there is no Black middle class as such. There are Black middle class individuals, but not class. For their children, the dislocation between our race and our color and our place where we are appears at times unshakable. Those who have been in France or Germany for generations are still called immigrants.

On that note, Mr. Chairman, I will end with a conversation I had with an older man in Edinburgh while I was at university about 8 or 9 years ago, who asked me where I was from. "Stevenage," I said. "But where were you born?" "Hitchen," I said, which is the town next door to Steven. "Well, before that," he asked. "Well, there was no before I was born," I said. "Well, where are your parents from?" "Barbados," I said. "Well, you're from Barbados, then," he said. "No," I said, "I'm from Stevenage."

Mr. HASTINGS. Very poignant. Thank you very much.

Assistant Secretary Commissioner Kramer, I'll turn to you for any questions you may pose to our witnesses.

Sec. KRAMER. Chairman, thank you.

My sincere thanks to both witnesses for very powerful presentations here this morning.

If I may, let me ask you to survey the situation in Europe, which country do you see as or consider providing the most protection from the wave of discriminatory movements that we read about, hear about, live within Europe? Which countries do you see as providing the greatest protections for non-White communities in the European continent? Which ones could be viewed as models in the European Union?

Dr. FRANS. Thank you, Commissioner Kramer.

The question—trying to point out which country provides the greatest protection is a difficult one to answer in the sense that on the face of it, all countries of the European Union have adequate protection constitutionally, institutionally and otherwise.

So it is a difficult one to answer, and the communities are also concentrated in different places but let me say this. Those countries that I see acknowledging the graveness of the issue would certainly be Holland on the one side.

I see that there's a lot of discussion in the United Kingdom, where the Black community is a very strong one, and also showing that the Council for Racial Equality was created and the Race Act was also enacted a long time ago.

This is also where there are big concentrations of Black people. Suddenly, in the country in which I live and work—Sweden—I think there is also some protection.

The answer would be that there are bits and pieces here and there, but on the whole, a lot needs to be done everywhere.

Dr. YOUNGE. I would largely agree with Mr. Frans in terms of the [inaudible] protection is everywhere and de facto there is a great deal of flux. Holland has traditionally been one of the better places, and yet in the last, I would say, 4 or 5 years there has been an alarming rise in xenophobia.

And one of the particular aspects of the Black experience in Europe is that it's very difficult to remove it from the broader non-White immigrant experience. So when Islamophobia is on the rise, there is going to be a general rising of racism and xenophobia.

There are places where there are stronger Black communities and where there are more liberal—Britain would be one of those, and Holland would be one of those—and then there are places where there is a more liberal mindset that makes it easier and most of Scandinavia I would camp in that.

In the last 4 years or 5 years there has been such a huge degree of flux—Denmark being a good example, with the cartoons of Mohammed—that it has become a moving target.

In general what I would say in Europe is that we think we're at a stage where it has generally been recognized by the constitution or institutionally and politically that racism is bad. It has yet to be acknowledged that anti-racism is good as the antidote. So moving from one state to the other is the moment that we're in here.

Sec. KRAMER. If I could ask you, Mr. Frans, you're a former member of the Swedish Parliament. I'm curious about the level of political participation in the Black communities throughout Europe. How would you describe it? Active? Not very active?

Dr. FRANS. Oh, very low. I think that there are individual islands of Black citizens here and there but generally, political participation is very low and you'd find one or two people here and there, but the inclusion in the mainstream politics of Black people is something that is still in its very embryonic status, I would say.

Those who say that recently, because of the triangular shift in policy from some political parties, many political parties in Europe have shied away in embracing popular participation, they are told, so as to attract a wider public.

The number of Blacks going into politics and being part of the political and trying to shape the political agenda is growing. So you may want to differentiate also from political participation in terms of voting, as opposed to representing the whole and being part of the agenda creating.

Voting—obviously, there is a trend. It is lower than the host communities or the White communities in Europe but it is actually very high in some communities. But political participation is not only voting. It's much more than that.

Sec. KRAMER. One more, if I may, Mr. Chairman, to Mr. Younge, if I can, particularly as a journalist—the role of the media and how you'd describe that.

Dr. YOUNGE. It has generally been quite inflammatory. The best example, really, is the Jyllands-Posten in Denmark. Now, some of the back-story, which is they published these cartoons of Mohammed. What was not widely known is that the year and a half before, they had turned down a similar set of cartoons about Jesus at Easter because they say it would upset the Christian leadership.

It can still sell papers. It had to be packaged in a certain way, but asylum seekers in particular and the framing of non-White people as immigrants and criminals is still very common.

The underlying message from the media is that there is an immigrant problem, but immigrant doesn't necessarily mean people who moved only recently.

Conversely, for almost every trend that you can say is getting worse, you will find a kind of undercurrent, which is not as strong, but nonetheless encouraging. It's been getting better.

Suddenly, in Britain, which is the journalistic culture I know best, there is an increase in non-White journalists. There's been an increase in Muslim journalists in particular.

I believe that is becoming true in other countries and also, if you take the wider media—particularly if you take literature—there has been a kind of real renaissance of Black writing in Europe, which is also encouraging in an age where actually lots of people don't read newspapers.

Ms. LEE. Thank you very much.

Mr. Frans, good morning. Let me ask you about the United Nations Working Group on People of African Descent. Could you talk a little bit about who's involved on this working group, if there is African American participation? Oftentimes and historically, some of us remember Malcolm X talking about African Americans having a presence at the United Nations.

I believe—and I'm not sure if this is still the case—that the NAACP for a while had a presence at the United Nations and I've often thought that it made a lot of sense for people of African descent in America to come together at the United Nations with other people of African descent to work on our common agenda to address the issues head-on from a global perspective, and I'd like to find out a little bit more about that from your position a vice chair.

Dr. FRANS. Thank you, Ms. Lee.

The Working Group on People of African Descent is a working group that will need much more support from people of African descent around the world. I believe that there are some African American organizations that participate, but the level of participation is absolutely too low and we could do much better.

We need a lot of support. We've done quite a lot of working, looking at the access to justice and making recommendations on how to come to terms with housing policies to increase integration. We've done work on education, and so we've done quite a lot and presented a lot of recommendations.

But at our working group meetings, which are open to the general public and to all organizations, I find that the program is that because of the cost involved, most civil society organizations oftentimes do not have the possibility of participating. So what I have been proposing over the last year is that maybe the working group should be traveling to and holding these meetings in other places instead.

But, of course, that would depend upon invitations from the states and this is a situation where the working group cannot travel to countries by itself, but needs to be invited. We have sent out a request to the states to be invited, and we are waiting. The only country that has been forthcoming has been Belgium and we've visited Belgium and any other member states that invite us we will be more than happy to travel and hold these in.

Ms. LEE. So you're actually housed now at the United Nations in New York?

Dr. FRANS. We're based in Geneva.

Ms. LEE. You're based in Geneva. OK, you're based then in Geneva actually. OK, OK.

Dr. FRANS. Technically speaking, we need to be invited to a country, to a member state, in order to be able to hold our meetings in that country.

Ms. LEE. OK.

Well, Mr. Chairman, maybe we could talk about this as a followup. I think it would be very interesting.

Mr. HASTINGS. Would you yield just one moment on that point?

Ms. LEE. Yes, I will.

Mr. HASTINGS. What's your funding structure? And how much are we talking about?

Dr. FRANS. The funding structure is voluntary contributions to the Office of the High Commissioner and there are five experts of the working group, so actually the cost of bringing together the working group itself is not so high. It has been difficult for civil society organizations to travel to Geneva and stay there for a couple of days, and that has been a problem.

There is no trust fund or other mechanisms of a trust fund where they can fund civil societies' participation. We do not have that, and so that is the problem.

Ms. LEE. It's very important work, and I look forward to working with you, Mr. Chairman, on the followup to this.

May I ask Mr. Younge one question?

Again, good morning. Where are you living now? Where are you from?

Dr. YOUNGE. I live in New York now.

Ms. LEE. You do live in New York.

Dr. YOUNGE. I'm the New York correspondent.

Ms. LEE. OK, OK. I wanted to ask you—in Europe, though, with regard to the role of religion and, of course, we're talking now in our own country with regard to the Christian religion coming from the Black experience, emanating, of course, from slavery, oppression. All of the issues that African Americans historically have addressed, of course, are manifested in the Black church.

How is religion addressed, for instance, in England now in terms of African descent? Is the Church of England, the Anglican Church, the main church where Black people attend? Or how do people bring forth their own experience through their religious background?

Dr. YOUNGE. First of all, I would say that religion plays a different role in Britain, so it's not as front and center as it can be in Black American politics. It doesn't draw so much of a political class from religion, because paradoxically, given that we have an established church, religion in general plays a much less kind of stock role in Britain.

In terms of the breakdown, I would say that most Black Britons are some form of Protestant, whether that's Anglican or not, so there's a large increase in Pentecostal and those kinds of religions. That's particularly true among those of African descent, as opposed to Afro-Caribbean descent.

If there's a development, then that's where it's coming from, the increase in the kind of new churches—Pentecostal churches—which are on the rise. But in general they play a far less significant role in our political lives than it does here.

Ms. LEE. I see. So you wouldn't say that there is a Black church movement or there's a Black church in England or anything in Europe?

Dr. YOUNGE. No and there are individual Black church leaders, who have played significant political roles. I'm thinking of Reverend Wilfred Wood and Bishop John Sentamu. Reverend Wood was the first Black Anglican bishop. So there are individuals who play significant roles, but not movements as such, as there are here.

Dr. FRANS. Mr. Chairman, I just wanted to add that it is true that people of African descent in Europe generally now, of course, are organizing themselves oftentimes around Pentecostal churches and this paradoxically plays two roles.

On the one hand, it plays the role of making integration harder in the sense that people get together. On the other hand, it plays the role of helping make integration better, you get together, identify what you want to achieve, see the issues you share in common and go on.

It is increasing. In Germany, in Holland, in Sweden and also in England, you have large congregations that are now beginning to buildup. For example, in Sweden now there is the Christian Council of Black Churches, which has been organizing itself. There is one in Germany, and there is one in Holland.

So there is some sort of a movement, and I would say that I agree with Mr. Younge that it is the Pentecostal churches that are taking the lead there. Also, the Bishop of Europe is from Uganda.

Ms. LEE. OK. Thank you very much.

Thank you, Mr. Chairman.

Mr. HASTINGS. Thank you, Ms. Lee.

Mr. Butterfield?

Mr. BUTTERFIELD. Thank you, Mr. Chairman.

Again, I thank both of you for coming today. It's been very informative, and I must confess to you that I have not read all of the material, and so I am at somewhat of a disadvantage and so I just want to ask you some very basic questions.

Tell me, if you will, what the Black presence in Europe is. Could you quantify it for me and give me an estimated number in all of Europe, East and West Europe? Was that a good question to ask?

Dr. FRANS. No and yes. Yes, no. East and West Europe makes it complicated in the sense that with West Europe, those countries of the European Union have some degree of data collection, and so you have it in the Eurostat and those figures are generally 2 or 3 years old, so 3.3 million is the official figure you'd receive, but we know that if you add now, then, East Europe and then also add the number of people who we call the sans papier, people without legal documents, then you'll be getting up to 4 or 5 million, even.

Mr. BUTTERFIELD. Under either approach, it's a small minority within Europe. Would that be a correct statement?

Dr. FRANS. Well, it would be a correct statement. In England it would be somewhere between 2 and 4 percent.

Two and 4 percent—is that the significant figure?

Dr. YOUNGE. All right. For people of African descent, it's that point.

Mr. BUTTERFIELD. And would you make a comparison between East and West? Where is the concentration?

Dr. FRANS. So the concentration of people of African descent, or Blacks, in Europe generally——

Mr. BUTTERFIELD. Eastern Europe.

Dr. FRANS. Eastern Europe—I would say maybe Czechoslovakia, of course the former Soviet republics used to have a lot of Black people who were studying there. Most of them have moved, but they remain focused, and there are still students there also.

Mr. BUTTERFIELD. With respect to those who are active and participate politically, who participate by voting, are there any legal or structural problems that you can tell us about that prevent full participation in the political process?

Dr. FRANS. In Europe as a whole?

Mr. BUTTERFIELD. In Europe as a whole. Are there impediments to voting, as we saw in this country 35 years ago?

Dr. FRANS. No, I mean constitutionally, I think——

Mr. BUTTERFIELD. I'm sure you know American history. You know about the literacy tests that we had 40 years ago and all of that. Are there problems here?

Dr. FRANS. No, I think generally we have good frameworks. Now, we get into the discussion of how you define impediments. In Denmark, for example, the inspection of Danish tests to become a citizen—would that be an impediment? Yes, I would say, because if you don't pass the test, you may not be granted citizenship.

And so, certainly, impediments from the fact that there is the unemployment, the racial profiling, and all that impacts on people in a sense that it impacts on them socially and psychologically in that they may decide not to take part.

Structurally, I don't think that there are impediments in that sense.

Dr. YOUNGE. I would just say one slightly different way of understanding the concentration is in a smaller sense, because it's almost entirely urban. So London, for example. One in 4 people in London are not White. Oxford—I would say about 16 percent, 1 in 6, would be of African descent.

So if you go to the major cities—Paris, London, Frankfurt, Hamburg—it would be almost impossible to avoid them. If you go to the countryside, then you may not know that anything's changed over the last 30 or 40 years but in the major cities, it's a sizable, significant number.

Mr. BUTTERFIELD. Among those who actually participate and vote in the electoral process, is there some degree of cohesion among those of African descent? Or is their political viewpoint fractured and splintered?

Dr. YOUNGE. For the most part, they would lean toward the liberal left—for the most part. That said, in England not quite to the extent that African Americans lean toward the Democratic Party in America, but that's probably because in Europe there are more parties but on the whole, to the liberal left.

Mr. BUTTERFIELD. One thing we've learned in this country is when you're in the minority, cohesion becomes absolutely important politically.

Dr. FRANS. It's correct, because typically you have four or five parties, even seven, in any given country and therefore, you don't see that and also the concentration of Black people in the cities makes it also quite obvious that in those areas that they lead, they have some sort of influence on the agenda of the political parties.

Mr. BUTTERFIELD. I think I'm about to run out of time. My final question to you is, are there significant outreach efforts from Black organizations in Western Europe with Black populations in Eastern Europe among the organizations and the people of Eastern Europe? Is there any outreach or any type of organized activity?

Dr. FRANS. Organized—I would say no.

Mr. BUTTERFIELD. OK.

Dr. FRANS. That would be the shortest answer. However, I would say that in the discussions that are centered around the European Network Against Racism, also in the discussion that is centered around the African Diaspora Policy Center, there are discussions on that.

Mr. BUTTERFIELD. Let me encourage that to continue.

Thank you, Mr. Chairman. I yield back.

Mr. HASTINGS. Thank you very much, Mr. Butterfield.

I'm going to forego questioning the two of you. I consider your testimony to be most poignant and critical for the establishment of this record.

Dr. Frans, if nothing more, I have gathered from this, particularly in light of Ms. Lee's question, the great need we have here at the Helsinki Commission to work more with the working group. I believe that there are opportunities. We are not necessarily any greater resourced, but at the same time might be able to bring to bear some hearings.

One that comes to mind would be to have something similar to this in yet another of the countries and to work with you in trying to get more of them to ask us on board.

Showing continuing interest in the subject, of course, we've been joined by the chairlady of the Congressional Black Caucus from Michigan, my dear friend and colleague, Congresswoman Carolyn Kilpatrick.

And following her is the Ranking Member of the Helsinki Commission, just joining us this moment, who has spent a considerable amount of his career dealing in a tangential way with a similar subject. He deals specifically with matters that are germane to those who are trafficked, particularly women and children, which comes in this same aegis in yet another way. So you would find him on record in patterns of migration in Europe and the things that do not speak well for overall society. He has tracked that.

Additionally, a member who is not with us, but has an interest, is Hilda Solis, who has the portfolio in the Parliamentary Assembly of dealing with migration.

But Chairman Kilpatrick and Commissioner Smith, if you would have anything you would like to say before I call up the next panel, I'd appreciate it.

HON. CAROLYN C. KILPATRICK (D–13) A MEMBER OF CONGRESS FROM THE STATE OF MICHIGAN

Ms. KILPATRICK. Thank you, Mr. Chairman and thank you for your foresight and your leadership—Helsinki couldn't be better with your stay there; thank you so much—and for calling us together today. I had a meeting in my district this morning before I could fly out, so I am happy to join you. Please forgive my tardiness.

I don't have a question at this time, sir. I just wanted to thank you and thank the panelists. We are going to build a record—the Congressional Black Caucus specifically, but the Democratic caucus in general, as witnessed by the committee. We have this jurisdiction, and I'm very interested in better relationships and ties.

We believe that the world is global. Two clicks of the mouse, and you can be anywhere. We no longer have to go from country to country and we want to build that, to build a better world, a safer world for God's children. Thank you very much.

Thank you, Mr. Chairman.

HON. CHRISTOPHER H. SMITH, RANKING MEMBER, COMMISSION ON SECURITY AND COOPERATION IN EUROPE

Mr. SMITH. Thank you very much, Mr. Chairman. I want to thank you for holding this hearing. I would ask unanimous consent that my statement be made a part of the record.

I welcome our witnesses. I apologize. I didn't get to hear your testimonies, but I will look at them later on.

I did want to just note, and I appreciate you bringing up the fact, that there are modern day slave routes going, especially from places like Nigeria into Rome and into other areas in Europe.

I have been to a number of shelters in Rome itself, where Nigerian girls are being sold like human chattel. It was outrageous. Thankfully, there were people on the scene, both government police, as well as non-governmental organizations, seeking to rescue these women.

I also was able to visit a number of shelters in Lagos and Abuja and was really touched by how robust those efforts were, but also how inadequate the funding and the resourcing was for those girls.

There were a number of Nigerian girls, and these were the lucky ones, who actually made their way back from Europe, and to hear them tell their stories was heartbreaking in the extreme and so I think that is a part of the degrading, and it's a form of racism, certainly. It certainly is a misogynistic view when it comes to women.

I want to thank you for what you're doing. And again, Mr. Chairman, this Commission has been, I think, talking for years, starting in the Parliamentary Assembly in St. Petersburg, Russia, in the late 1990s, on the issue of human trafficking.

Hopefully, the lessons learned from chattel slavery in the United States, as new forms of slavery manifest themselves, will be learned and combated with extreme prejudice in the positive way—fighting it.

Mr. HASTINGS. Thank you very much, Chris.

Gentlemen, thank you. Please stay, if you can.

We will call up our second panel now: Dr. Philomena Essed from Antioch University, The Netherlands Equal Treatment Commission; and Dr. Allison Blakely, author and historian from Boston University; and Dr. Clarence Lusane, the International Race Politics author at American University.

I'm particularly pleased now that Dr. Blakely and Drs. Lusane and Essed are here and Dr. Blakely—we had it up; I don't know; the map that's not there—but Dr. Blakely has done the immense studies on where the numbers are. And so, G.K., I think he would be able to empiricize for you on many of those matters.

I'd like to start with Dr. Essed, and as I said with reference to the other witnesses, their extraordinary curriculum vitae and biographies are on the table outside, and I invite persons who are with us to pick them up, as they see fit.

Dr. Essed, if you would like to start, please, ma'am?

PHILOMENA ESSED, ANTIOCH UNIVERSITY, THE NETHERLANDS, EQUAL TREATMENT COMMISSION

Dr. ESSED. Thank you, Mr. Chairman for inviting me to this hearing. My written statement made for the occasion, called "An ABC on People of African Descent in Europe", consists of an alphabetically organized list of content areas that might be relevant and useful for understanding experiences and conditions of people of African descent in Europe.

Here, I will highlight just a few items from the list in view of further discussion and questions you may have.

The first letter I would like to point to is the "i" of Identity. Even when you can formally categorize 3 to 5 million people in Europe as of Afro descent, not all identify as such.

Many identify not often even in terms of color or race, but in terms of the country they came from or the country they migrated to. This is an important difference compared to African Americans.

It should be noted in this respect that there are also many African Americans in Europe, tourists, students, in particular in the cosmopolitan cities.

The "c" of Colonialism: for many people of Afro descent, the historical contexts of reference are colonialism and post-colonialism, rather than slavery, even when they might be descendants of enslaved Africans, as people from Caribbean are of American background.

Many came to the so-called motherlands in Europe with European passports—for instance, people from Surinam and the Dutch Antilles; the French from Martinique.

Colonialism, its economic, social and psychological implications and consequences, are largely ignored in European countries. Colonial relations, however, continue to exist, including the inequalities involved. For instance, the Dutch Antilles are still colonies, and they are a popular tourist attraction for mostly White Dutch.

For the local population, the reality is different. Extremely high unemployment numbers in the Dutch Antilles, unrealistic ideas about "rich" lives in the Netherlands, or the desire to reunite with family members have caused high numbers to migrate to the Netherlands and that was the same for people from Surinam in the 1970s.

Insufficient care, social indifference, lack of schooling and job opportunities, racial prejudice and a sense of anonymity in the Netherlands contribute to violence and criminality among Antilleans, in particular young men.

In response, the Dutch state seems to entertain controversial and probably unlawful ethnic data bases on Antilleans, on the basis of which enhanced security and preventive law enforcement interventions can take place.

Among Antillean women, teenage pregnancies are a problem, often a result of a combination of factors, including physical or emotional abandonment at home, racial discrimination and ignorance.

To conclude briefly on the issue of colonialism, the consequences of colonialism have not been dealt with in Europe. I am referring to dependency mentality, and a sense of powerlessness among formerly colonized.

But neither has been addressed the remnants of European colonial mentality, the paternalism and the creation of second-class citizens, which happened in the U.K., and which is happening in the Netherlands as well as in France.

This brings me to the "e" of Everyday Racism. Racism is integrated in the routine practices of everyday European cultures and institutions, resulting in informally segregated neighborhoods, for instance, in the U.K., in France and in Germany.

Informally sanctioned segregated schools—the so-called Black and White schools—in the Netherlands are an example. In neighborhoods harassment of refugee families is not unusual. For instance, Spain or a recent case concerning a Liberian family in the Netherlands, where the local government was completely informed social workers were informed, but nobody was doing anything. Eventually, the family, desperate, had to leave the neighborhood.

There is police violence against people of African descent. Austria is a case in point.

Among the most damaging forms of everyday racism are those involving individuals in positions of authority, whose decision-making power has the potential of making and breaking school careers or professional opportunities.

Due to the public taboo, however, on mentioning racism and the emotional, if not aggressive, response to accusations of racism from the side of White Europeans, many Afro descendants are neither aware of racism, nor sufficiently equipped to resist. I'm saying many; I'm not saying all. Resilience and awareness can be a function of whether and how people are involved—for instance, in community activism.

Frequently, those exposed to racism experience powerlessness in the face of the accusation that they are just oversensitive. The degree of denial of everyday racism can hardly be overestimated in Europe.

We need to address the impact of racism on the lives of Black and brown people in Europe. This should be an issue for European policymakers as well.

The "f" of Fortress Europe—increasingly tight borders since the signing of the treaty are not preventing economic and war refugees from risking their lives in search of a better future in Europe. Many die prematurely in the passage between North Africa and southern Europe—young men, women and children.

In the meantime, middlemen are making blood money. The construction of illegality has different impacts on men and women. Little is known about the particular conditions of illegal immigrants who try to survive as street vendors, mostly male, mostly in southern Europe; as domestics, mostly women; or in prostitution, mostly women but also including young Moroccan men.

Which brings me to the "g" of Gender. Race is not gender neutral. Perceptions of Afro descendants—men and women—are shaped by many factors, including histories of colonialism, the "White male-native mistress" experience, imagined exoticism and Black women perceived as sensual and sexualy accessible and recurrent media images of African wars on poverty, highlighting male aggression. Of influence as well are stereotypical images of African Americans. U.S. media are global.

The sex trade and abuse of African women have been reported, among others, in Belgium. In the Netherlands, where prostitution is legal, women of Afro descent end up in the lowest paid and most risky sectors of sex work.

Beauty norms are another gender issue. Little is known in Europe about the impact of White beauty norms on women of Afro descent. For instance, skin bleaching has been found to be a problem among women of Ghanaian background in the Netherlands.

Circumcision of girls occurs among refugees from Somalia. Policymakers have not been successful in including the women of these communities, which is so important, in endeavors to put an end to this practice.

Finally, in schools, Afro descendant girls of Caribbean origin families—and it's a point that it's not all bad news—are outperforming male counterparts in the Netherlands. I think that is the case also in the U.K.

The percentage of highly educated women among the Afro-Caribbean Dutch is more or less equal to that of highly educated White Dutch women. This does not, however, translate into equal representation at higher levels on the labor market.

Mr. HASTINGS. Thank you so much, Dr. Blakely. I was going to come to you and ask Dr. Lusane, since he's younger-looking——

[Laughter.]

ALLISON BLAKELY, AUTHOR AND HISTORIAN, BOSTON UNIVERSITY

Dr. BLAKELY. Thank you, sir, and good morning. Chairman Hastings, other distinguished Commissioners and Members of Congress, ladies and gentlemen, I'd like to first add my expression of gratitude for your showing recognition of the seriousness and importance of this issue.

I've been researching this subject area now for some three decades, and so for me this is almost like a mirage, a dream come true, just to have this degree of attention from people such as yourselves.

As a historian and a comparative historian, my contribution to this discussion is, I think, going to be the most general. I'm looking at Europe as a whole. My doctorate is in Russian history, so I have a special interest in that part.

In diaspora studies, I really am looking at Europe as a whole. The history of Blacks in modern Europe is converging with the present situation to create an unprecedented level of Black population in Europe proper. The size and significance of this Black presence are not yet widely recognized, neither by scholars nor the general public.

I am the author of this map that you see coming and going up there [on the screen before you] at times. Those who don't happen to have a paper copy, I'd be glad to discuss it with you later.

My findings are that there is a population of over 5 million Blacks in Europe that can be documented closely with census data. My belief is that, in fact, there is probably something approaching, if not over, 1 percent of the total European population, which is around 750 million or so.

More importantly, the Black population is growing. If you don't believe that, take a tour of urban public schools. You'll see the same phenomenon that you see in our urban centers. You'll be startled in the case of Europe, because if there's only a half percent, as some are saying, why do you find the majority Blacks in some of the elementary school classes?

The answer is simple. Just look at the same phenomenon, the United States is experiencing with recently our State of California recording a less than 50 percent population level for the traditional White population. Texas is just on the horizon, and the numbers will grow.

There is declining population across Europe in terms of the traditional population. And so, in a sense, the handwriting is on the wall. You'll have a greater colored Europe of various cultural and colored complexions. It's just a question of how the Europeans are going to cope with it.

My one driving concern, in terms of the implications of the kind of research I've done, is that Europe may—I hope they don't—but they may resort to that old tried and proven Black identity as one way of establishing what would be a cheap labor force in the future, even in a society where the Black population does increase to a point where no one will say that it's insignificant.

I am also concerned, because recently the Islamic vs. Western cultural clash has tended to overshadow this other, more long-standing kind of cultural clash just as well.

Literally, some of the individuals and groups in what would be the traditionally defined Black population may fall through the cracks because of the lack of special interest because of this other admittedly extremely important other kind of cultural clash that's taking place.

One thing that I have concluded is that finally the European Black population has reached a level where some comparisons might be made with the Black American experience. Ideally, I would hope that they may learn from some of our mistakes and decide against repeating those.

For centuries, millions of Black African descent people were subjected to domination in the leading European colonial empires; but technically in Europe now, is that in these European democracies, those former colonials are being brought in and supposedly integrated into a situation where they should at least have equal opportunity.

That kind of a transition is not easy in human affairs, where the lines were clearly understood of hierarchy based on color and wealth and power in the colonies; and now suddenly the Europeans—in some cases, who have tended to think that those colonials had nothing to do with them—now, because of labor shortages and so on, they're having to learn to live with the former colonial people, who are subjects or citizens.

The kinds of comparisons that I'm alluding to with the Black American experience can be seen in the fact that if you look at the recent outbreak of violence in France a couple of years ago, especially, the kinds of issues that have been identified as explaining that kind of outbreak, they read just like the Kerner Commission report or the Scarman report about similar violence in the 1980s in England.

So there's no mystery here that some of the same elements, same dynamics are potentially there. I would also point out that the

American-style ghetto may not be as visible in European society, but it definitely is there.

For 4 months at the end of last year, I was in Europe and deliberately visiting predominantly Black neighborhoods in Lisbon and London, France, and the Netherlands and I even looked into the history in Hamburg, which is an especially interesting case. Although they don't look the same, many of the same kinds of problems are in these different countries. Their potential dangers, if not already manifest, need to be dealt with.

A major component in all of this is the legacy of negative stigmatization of blackness and the stereotypes that have come down to us from that, that are still very much with us. You only need to look a little bit below the surface in the media and other aspects of European, as well as American, culture to see.

What I am raising is the question of whether even now in the 21st century we can get beyond those kinds of stereotypes. I'm really encouraged by the fact that you have Lady Valerie Amos, who has served as the head of the House of Lords in England.

We know what we celebrate in this country in terms of visibility of Blacks in much higher places and so on and yet in Europe you have multimillion-dollar soccer players having to experience having bananas thrown at them on the field and racial epithets. So just because there may be some progress on one level doesn't mean that the problems have gone away.

I conclude that the main reason that the image and status of Blacks continues to suffer is economic. I don't think there's any kind of innate belief in the dominant society that Blacks are inferior. I think that this kind of notion has been reinforced over the centuries mainly for economic reasons.

First, to justify the slave trade and the employment of slave labor. Now, because these are the images that sell—the media, advertising industry, sports—that's what sells. That's what's profitable, and that's what keeps it going. Otherwise, I think we could escape from some of this over a generation or two. But as long as there is that economic motivation underpinning all of this, I think we have a problem.

There are many questions ongoing: Are those stereotypes of Blacks still relevant? Or am I just kind of a dinosaur, still talking about things that don't exist anymore? Are people of Black African descent in Europe considered European? Or are they still considered primarily Black?

How do Black people—people I'm calling Black—self-identify in Europe? That's a very important consideration. The question of solidarity has been raised. My sense is that there would be a tendency not to even want to seek solidarity.

I'm descended from sharecroppers in Green County, Alabama; before that, slaves. My ancestors didn't define themselves as Black either. That was something that was imposed on them.

What I'm sensing about now is that the Europeans might have a chance to skip that stage and move on into true integration without all the fuss; but because of the way economic conditions are conspiring against that, I'm just not sure that's going to happen.

I am encouraged by all the Europe-wide organizations, the national human rights organizations, and so on. That may help. We did some of this.

But in my own area of specialization, for example—Russia—I've had to cancel recent trips, because friends have warned me, "Just don't go." I can't ride the metro. I can't go out by myself anymore.

I first visited Russia in '65, and I was safer under Soviet Communism—for the wrong reason. They protected with the police state, and they wanted foreign currency, and so they rigidly enforced protection of individuals.

Now there is no motivation anymore to protect Black people— neither Black orphans from the tens of thousands of Africans who were there and have now gone, not just Black visitors, male or female.

A more authoritarian regime there now, in some ways, than in recent years, has clamped down on the media, so there's not even active reporting anymore of all the victimization that has taken place. Although the government recently—I think it was Hitler's birthday—did provide the African students with provisions so that they could stay off the streets for that period, because in Eastern Germany and in Russia in particular, that's the way it is at present.

I'll conclude my formal presentation now. I'll be glad to engage in any questions.

Mr. HASTINGS. Thank you, Dr. Blakely and I note that you were going through your prepared statement, and I'd invite you to, after your summarization, include your full statement in the record.

Then I would say to our audience, as well as all of you, we will continue a full report regarding this matter. I have the misfortune of having an appointment at 11:30 and Dr. Lusane, I mean no offense. I'll leave during the course of your presentation.

I also apologize to my fellow Commissioners and our colleagues and ask them to please stay. The Ranking Member has indicated, our friend Chris Smith, that he will conclude the proceedings for us.

I invite you to our Web site, those of you that are interested, and I can say unequivocally, Dr. Frans, you will hear from us, and Gary Younge, as well as all of you. We owe you a debt of gratitude.

I did not ask any questions. I would send to you, and ask for your followup for our report, any question that I may have, if you would present it to us in writing.

Dr. Lusane?

CLARENCE LUSANE, INTERNATIONAL RACE POLITICS AUTHOR, AMERICAN UNIVERSITY

Dr. LUSANE. Thank you. Good morning, Chairman Hastings and honorable men and women of the Commission, as well as to our audience and to my colleagues.

I want to echo the sentiments that have been stated and also thank the commission for providing this historic and what some would even say is earth-shaking opportunity to discuss what is emerging as one of the most important issues confronting the future of Europe: the status and means of social inclusion of people of African descent.

For more than 20 years, I've worked with minority communities and NGOs in Europe, including people of African descent, focused on issues of human rights, immigration, racial equalities, and intolerance.

Similar to Congresswoman Lee, I also had the wonderful opportunity to live in England for a number of years, and that work included a number of years working as Assistant Director of the 1990 trust of Black human rights organizations based in the U.K.

In that capacity I worked with governments, regional institutions, such as the European Union and the Council of Europe, around these concerns. I also would note that I wrote a book called Hitler's Black Victims, which looks at the experiences of people of African descent under Nazism, which I will also submit to the Commission for the official record.

Although the oldest skull ever found in Europe belonged to an African, and even though African Americans have been in England since at least the late 1800s, for most people in Europe, a settled presence of Black people is viewed as a relatively new phenomenon.

In fact, there have been several waves of Blacks in Europe since the end of World War II. In England, France, the Netherlands and other countries, Black migration was critical to the rebuilding of Europe. Waves of Blacks came to Western Europe to drive the buses, to nurse the sick and to sweep the streets of the great cities of that region.

In Eastern Europe Communists states from Russia to Poland to the former Yugoslavia welcomed African students, scholars, artists, and other professionals as part of an effort to aid liberation movements in newly independent states. These new populations merged with older and smaller Black communities.

However, in both Western and Eastern Europe, Blacks and other minorities were never fully integrated into the society. The evidence is overwhelming.

First, they have often been the targets of violent racist attacks. As my colleague just mentioned, in Russia and a number of places, skinheads and neo-fascist organizations in Russia, Austria, Germany, and other states have specifically targeted Blacks, and a number of individuals have been murdered in recent years.

In fact, according to research by Searchlight magazine, a number of these organizations also have direct links with racist and neo-fascist organizations in the United States, including even the Ku Klux Klan.

Second, there remain persistent disparities in the social arena. In housing, education, health care and other areas, Blacks in Europe are at or near the bottom. In the U.K., which is one of the few countries in Europe that actually keeps statistics, Black students are failed at two to three times the rate of White European students.

Blacks have an unemployment rate that's 18 percent lower than the general population and Blacks are 50 percent more likely to die of a stroke. As you will note, these statistics are similar to the statistics facing many African Americans in this country.

Third, racial issues are also acute in the realm of criminal justice. Police violence, deaths in custody, and disproportionate incarcerations are major concerns in England, France, Spain, Germany, Italy, and a number of other states in the region.

Again, in the U.K. Black people are six times more likely to be stopped and searched by the police and three times more likely to be arrested than Whites. In France police-Black community tensions sparked the deadly riots that occurred in 2005.

The racialization of crime and the criminalization of a race are both having devastating impacts on Black communities in Europe.

Fourth, Blacks are also suffering from the harsh, unfair, and discriminatory immigration policies that exist in the region. Anti-discrimination sentiments are rampant and are not just restricted to the far right. In fact, not only are conservative parties adopting these positions, but so are formerly social democratic parties.

There are a number ways outside of this to move beyond these conditions.

First, it is important that states begin to collect social and economic data on the situations of racial and ethnic minorities in the region. Understandably, the history of Nazism, fascism and ethnic cleansing has generated a reluctance to gather racial data, but the lack of the empirical data continues to hamper the development of concrete policies that can effectively address the social exclusion of Europe's minorities.

This is also relevant to the issue of, as my colleague mentioned earlier, identifying how people of African descent in Europe actually see themselves.

There are a number of different categories of people of African descent. There are those who are citizens, for example, and those who have become citizens in a number of different ways.

Some were born in Europe and became citizens. Some have become naturalized citizens. You even have those who were adopted, for example, from Brazil and a number of other places, who have dual citizenship. You have those who are legal residents, who aren't citizens, who may be in the categories of asylum seekers or refugees and then you also have those who are undocumented.

So all of these are important statistics to gather so that there is a realistic understanding and sense of what the demography of people of African descent actually constitute, as well as there are ways to find out how people identify themselves.

Second, there's a need to strengthen the content and enforcement of anti-discrimination laws and policies. The 2000 race directive from the European Union provided a foundational framework for constructing policies that can address discrimination. However, the legislation only covers EU member states and is only focused on anti-racism.

Legislation must begin to address the issue of racial equity and means by which progress can be made to close the disparities that currently exist and are growing.

Third, along these lines it's critical to establish effective and empowered government agencies that are focused on anti-discrimination and anti-racism. These entities should be built in such a manner that they maintain independence from political parties and narrow government interests.

The United Nations has outlined specific guidelines in creating these types of independent government-related bodies.

Last, and perhaps most urgent, there is a need to include the voices of Black communities in development of anti-discrimination and anti-racism and equality policies. A wide range of Black and anti-racist NGOs have developed over recent years, but have too often been excluded from the policy debates that are critical to the communities that they seek to represent.

Thank you.

Mr. SMITH. Thank you very much for your testimonies and for being here.

This is an historic hearing. To the best of my knowledge, we have not had a hearing that's so focused on the experience of Africans in Europe, so I think your testimonies will become part, I think, of a record that will be read very widely.

So thank you again for the contributions you are making to the knowledge of the Commission and hopefully toward mitigating and ending racism forever. And it certainly is a dream that all of us have.

Let me ask, first, Dr. Blakely, I looked at your map, and again, I appreciate your testimony. You note that in France there are some 2.5 million Africans in France.

We ran into a real problem, on the whole issue of anti-Semitism in France as well, in the collection of data. There was a reluctance almost like a wall, and it seems to me if you want to combat a long evil, you need to collect data, and you need to be as specific as possible.

We found that on the anti-Semitic issue that when swastikas appeared on gravestones that had been overturned in Jewish cemeteries or are on places of worship, it was just dismissed as hooliganism. So a lot of us pressed very hard that you need to collect data to adequately combat a crime and to categorize it as a hate crime for what it is.

I'm wondering what your experience has been, if you could, on the whole issue of France and this reluctance to collect that kind of data.

Let me ask Dr. Essed—is that the way it's said?

In the Netherlands we have an ongoing argument with the Dutch Government, since they have legalized prostitution. Amsterdam certainly has large numbers of women who are being degraded and exploited each and every day in their brothels.

There was one rapporteur who suggested that upwards of 80 percent of those women are foreign born and also are there through coercion or deception. They had not gone there voluntarily, even though if you talked to them in a way that is not in a safe place, where they might be fearful of retaliation, they'll say, "Oh, I'm here voluntarily," but that's not the case. So many of these women are being exploited cruelly.

So my question would be what has been your experiencing in pushing back? It seems to me that prostitution and the line of demarcation between that and trafficking of women for sexploitation is very, very thin indeed, and that there are many women who are right on that line, and they certainly are being exploited, and that ought to be a cause of concern.

Finally, a question about what I consider to be an active racism that happens all over the world. It happened in the United States and it has in large part its genesis in writings that began at the same time that the Germans were beginning their eugenics movement and racial politics, the Aryan race and all of the hate that came out of that.

Margaret Sanger is the founder of Planned Parenthood, and unbeknownst to large numbers of people—I've read many of her books; one of her books is called The Pivot of Civilization—in it she has a chapter that's called "The Cruelty of Charity."

She talks—and I actually gave a floor speech on it recently—about how the new government program—and then a lot of philanthropists were getting involved with helping indigent women who were suffering from poverty, who were pregnant, and people were trying to provide maternal care to them—she saw that as cruelty. And she said it without any ambiguity in her writing.

She said, "Such benevolence is not merely superficial and near-sighted. It conceals a stupid cruelty. Aside from the question of the unfitness of many women to become mothers, aside from the very definite deterioration in the human stock that such programs would inevitably hasten, we may question its value even to the normal through unfortunate mothers. For it is never the intention of such philanthropy to give poor, overburdened and often undernourished mother of the slum the opportunity to make a choice for herself."

It goes on, "The most serious challenge that can be brought against modern benevolence is that it encourages the perpetuation of defectives, delinquents and dependents."

In the United States a woman who is African American is three times more likely to have an abortion—300 percent higher abortion rates than among Caucasians or even Latinos. In my State of New Jersey, for every three pregnancies, two are aborted of the African American, 40 percent for the Latinos, and about one-third are Caucasian.

I see it as a massive loss of babies' lives, as well as an exploitation of those women. But my question really goes to the heart of a bias that focuses on these vulnerable people. When we should be surrounding these women with love, compassion and outreached hands, they are being shown to an abortion clinic.

I'm wondering if the African experience—and before I ask, all of you might want to answer this—Dr. Alveda King, the niece of Dr. Martin Luther King, has had two abortions. Dr. King has spoken out very strongly that there is a racial tinge to all of this and has said, and I quote her: "How can a dream survive, if the children are murdered?"

So my question to you is is that something that is happening in Europe as well? My deep concern is for the babies. Whatever their color, they need to be protected and it seems to me that there's a disproportionality and a focus on African babies and the question would be is that also happening in Europe?

Dr. BLAKELY. Commissioner Smith, thank you for your question.

I'll address the one concerning France and the ethnic and racial designations. As a historian, this is very problematical, because, for example, if you go into the library and you try to do research, using the standard means, categories don't exist. You have to almost go in already knowing where what you're looking for is.

I should also preface my remarks, I guess, by saying that I have a tremendous amount of respect for France and its republican tradition, of which the French are very proud but I disagree strongly with their notion that if you don't name something, it doesn't exist.

Part of the practical problem—with the attitude that we don't have ethnic categories—there's actually a law against having official categories—is when you have something like what occurred at the end of 2005, you don't even have a vocabulary to talk about it and that's very problematical.

I think France is not the only country in that category but there are ways of getting information—local social work organizations, for example, and in the communities themselves and their institutions but I think it's unfortunate that there isn't a greater acceptance of the necessity to at least acknowledge the true-to-life experiences of the people in order to address the needs of society as a whole.

Dr. LUSANE. Yes. I want to echo those comments, because it is a problem in Germany. It's a problem in Spain. It's a problem in Italy. It's a problem across the region. And it manifests itself at one level in just getting basic social statistics.

So, for example, is there a disproportionate number of people of African descent in the prisons? If you don't see that as a category, and you don't do that kind of counting, then you don't address the issue.

In the U.K., where they do keep this kind of accounting, there's a massively disproportionate number for Black women, for example, who constitute probably 2 to 3 percent of the population, constitute probably 20 percent or more of the prison population so that means that you can't just generally address the issue, but you specifically need to look at what's going on.

A similar case can be made in France, where independent researchers from the University of France and Sorbonne and some other places, have gone into the prisons and literally just counted people and found these kinds of disproportionalities but because the state itself doesn't collect this data, it becomes very difficult to develop policies.

It really is a regional problem, not just in France, and one that really is critical to develop any kind of policies that can address the disparities and discriminations that exist.

Dr. ESSED. I would briefly add that, for instance, in the Netherlands one can register where individuals or their parents are born which is an indirect way of registering race and ethnicity. Sometimes it's done voluntarily, and sometimes not. The numbers are often unreliable, and there are cases where researchers just counted "colored" faces—face value, basically.

I would like to address the issue you mentioned about abortion. I'm not aware that there is a special focus on people of African descent in relation to abortion.

What happens is that none of the countries, as far as I know, has been out to promote abortions, but to making something possible as a last resort, because I don't think there's any woman who likes to have an abortion in the sense of looking forward to that.

I think it's an awful experience—but sometimes women opt for abortion because they think an alternative would be even worse.

In countries where abortion was legalized, as in the Netherlands, the numbers dropped, and it has been dropping for decades. There are still concerns about the relatively higher number of abortions among immigrants, in particular from the Caribbean, from Morocco and Turkey, where many young people lack access to sex education.

Among the second generation born and raised in the Netherlands the abortion numbers are lower.

Mr. SMITH. Ms. Lee?

Ms. LEE. Thank you, Mr. Chairman. I don't want to continue this abortion debate, but I just want to say for the record some of us believe that a woman should have a right to privacy, a woman should have a right to choose, and the government should not interfere in decisions that are being made which should be made between a woman, her family and her health care provider.

And I just wanted to say many of us believe that part of what we have to do is provide comprehensive sex education at a very early age so that women and girls know how to protect themselves from getting pregnant and from the transmission of sexually transmitted diseases and infections.

Let me go to, I guess, Dr. Blakely and ask you with regard to the fact you mentioned the cheap labor now that's taking place in Europe with people of African descent. How does that factor in, in terms of the brain drain from especially Africa and the Caribbean?

It's my understanding that people working abroad, immigrants working abroad are remitting back maybe $45 billion a year to their home countries. However, the continent of Africa and, of course, the Caribbean still are underdeveloped. And so what's the relationship between cheap labor and the brain drain on the continent of Africa?

Dr. BLAKELY. Well, it's a very complicated question, as you know, Congresswoman Lee.

And my mind was racing as you were completing your question, because actually now another issue has just arisen, which is seeing in some instances Eastern Europe immigrants actually replacing Blacks in Europe as the cheap labor of choice, so to speak. And so that's another kind of factor that's beginning to show itself.

The other development is that the European countries have in recent years started restricting immigration and trying precisely to only accept people with real skills, with the kinds of skills that you might put under the category of a brain drain.

And it's a very difficult—at least at the moment—and insoluble problem, I think, for African countries, poor African countries, because things are in turmoil at home. The opportunities for those people to realize their dreams are not there at home. They prefer, I think, to stay in Africa. But as long as there are those opportunities in Europe, that really doesn't seem to be anything that's going to change.

Ms. LEE. Thank you very much. Let me followup and just ask——

Oh, did you have a response, Dr. Lusane?

Dr. LUSANE. Yes, I just wanted to add to that that the big paradox in Europe is that even as [inaudible] sentiments kind of arise, the reality is that Europe needs labor. And studies from the United Nations and the international labor organization studies done by the E.U. have shown that Europe will needs tens and tens and tens of millions of workers over the next 50 years, and they will come from the developing world.

There just are not going to be enough people coming from Eastern Europe, which is actually not all that welcome either. But certainly, there will be a big need.

So some of the forward thinkers in Europe, particularly at the European Union level, really are recognizing this, and so immigration policy really has to start to prepare itself for dealing with the new demographics that are necessary, given the aging population in Europe and the low birth rate among European Whites.

Ms. LEE. Thank you.

And, Dr. Essed, yes, did you have a response?

Dr. ESSED. Just to briefly answer this. It also should be seen in relation to the amount of money immigrants send back home. This is a source of development income for these countries. So I think it's complex, and there is some sort of balance.

South Africa is a different matter, but I'll not go into that, for the sake of time.

Ms. LEE. Thank you.

And just very quickly, what I'm hearing from all of you is because of the lack of data collection and statistical gathering and the fact that the numbers aren't quite there yet, we don't really know what the impact of racism and discrimination is, other than by knowing.

And so here in America, of course, we have had affirmative action policies that have helped in some ways to level the playing field, although now they're actually being eroded and turned around, and people now are being shut out of employment, contracting opportunities, opportunities for higher education.

In my State, for example, there was a proposition that totally eliminated affirmative action, so we're back to ground one.

In Europe is affirmative action seen as a possibility? Does it make sense, if in fact the numbers were ever there or the data was gathered to be able to begin to develop policies to turn some of these recognizable conditions around that we as African Americans feel and understand and live with every day here now?

Dr. ESSED. Can I reply? There has been some positive action, which is not exactly the same as affirmative action, but what it boils down to is the idea that if you have two applicants who are equally competent, then you take the applicant of color, that is, or the woman.

Positive action programs have been applied in the U.K. in the 1980s, and in the Netherlands in the 1980s as well. Research indicates that positive action did have some corrective impact on the more open forms of discrimination, but it certainly did not lead to any preference for Black candidates.

Dr. BLAKELY. One development that is occurring as things progress is that there are consciously Black organizations taking shape. For example, in France there is an organization—well, the acronym is CRAN. It's the representative council of Black associations.

Its leader, Patrick Lozes, is a pharmacist, has political aspirations, but he actually has carried out the first major survey a couple of years ago, both in terms of trying to get a more accurate population count and in terms of the kinds of issues that concern Black people.

He's consciously modeled his organization after the National Association for the Advancement of Colored People. He claims to have 300 chapters.

Ms. LEE. I really want to thank you for coming. This is the beginning of a long, historical journey that we must take to rebuild the world, and I appreciate your study, your professionalism and all of that.

As chair of the Congressional Black Caucus, I just want to give you a little data on us. We have 43 Members from 21 different States. We represent over 40 million Americans. Eighteen of our members represent less than 50 percent African Americans. Five percent of our members represent less than 15 percent. So we represent all of America.

We have millions more who are not represented by an African American, but who come to us and work with us from all over the country. We represent Latinos, Asians. We represent Europeans, Native Americans. The gamut is who we are as members of the Caucus, and we're proud to do that.

When Congressman Hastings talked about having this session and building a commonality that we might come to, it was to [inaudible] and most instructive. I always believed—and I'm a grandmother and an educator by profession—education is the equalizer in the world. It always has been and always will be.

Whenever you have good schools, and children and young people participate and grow, then they have more options, and not only their family, their community and the world is better. You all achieved that, and I'm sure that those you work with have, too.

And seeing the countries—we haven't really gotten into that now, but I hope we will, as we move forward—they, too, are the count to tens or others of color who have gone on to become professionals and educated.

Economics, the other "e," is also in America—education, economics—and it sounds like in other countries of the world, those are the two things that are the equalizers.

As chair of the Caucus, I'm here today to hear from you, and I thank you very much. And then I want to move the ball to how we go from here. What would you recommend—each of the three of you—that today—not only put on the record, but as members of the Caucus and the Democratic Congress, as well as the entire House of Representatives, what one or two things would you say we work on today?

Dr. ESSED. I would definitely say active and proactive anti-discrimination laws. Formally, things are in place, but the way it works out is not sufficient.

Even when there is, for instance, at least in the Netherlands, the reversal of the burden of proof, it remains very difficult to deal with cases where you have the kind of subtle racist acts that build-up from day to day and where it's the whole process, and not one thing that you can point to and "prove".

As an advisory body which also assists in implementing the anti-discrimination law the Dutch Equal Treatment Commission, is highly valuable, because often members of the judiciary have not really focused on issues of race. In addition, the Commission is fairly accessible as well for people without much formal education. But more needs to be done than the Commission alone can do.

Ms. LEE. How can we impact that? They're all independent states, independent governments. They're the E.U. They're the United Nations. They're the Congress. How do we interact internationally so it will impact that?

Dr. ESSED. Keeping at the European case to promote diversity, especially in the workplace. It's education and work. If you don't have jobs, you're damaging the future of generations. If you don't have education, you don't get jobs because of the increasingly higher requirements for obtaining work.

In the workplace racial discrimination is rampant in many of the European countries and it doesn't matter what your level of education is—you hit a glass ceiling. More cross-Atlantic cooperation might be helpful, for instance, in relation to the experience of African Americans, who might not be in the ideal situation, from what I hear, definitely not, but there is more experience in resisting racism. We can learn from the mistakes that have been made here and we can learn from the gains that have been made here.

Second, keep at the case of each and every European country. Is there diversity in the workplace? What example does the government display, in this respect? How many Black people are employed by the government?

Particular attention is needed for the protection of people of African descent in Eastern Europe, who are under physical attack every day.

Dr. BLAKELY. I think we do have to respect other nations' sovereignty, but on issues such as censorship, for example, such as I mentioned with Russia, I would think there is already acknowledgement that the new Russia may be leaning in the wrong direction right now with respect to true democracy.

If we could just keep that kind of issue on the table, encouraging our Russian allies to remember that there's supposed to be substance behind those kinds of ideals.

With respect to the question of encouraging more European countries to acknowledge that there may be a problem to address with respect to some of these issues—France or Germany, for example—there must be some polite way to sort of keep constant pressure to try to, if nothing else, use our example. Don't make the mistakes we did and don't be in denial about very real kinds of societal problems until you have violent explosions. That's not the way to deal with it.

Dr. LUSANE. Yes. I'm a very strong believer in people-to-people relations. And I think probably most critical is that we really need to look for our counterpart. I really want to thank you for your overview of the Congressional Black Caucus.

As you know and other members know, I believe it was probably little more than a decade ago, the Congressional Black Caucus was very critical in the launching of the Parliamentary Black Caucus in the U.K. Now, that experiment failed for a number of reasons, but the impulse behind it was important.

So there is a need for Black elected officials in the United States to be in touch with Black elected officials and aspiring Black elected officials in the U.K. I tell my students all the time, they need to be in touch with students over there.

So we need that kind of ongoing exchange, that ongoing dialogue, so that we are learning from each other's experiences.

Second, I think we raise that to a more strategic level when we look at a number of issues. When I was in the U.K., one of the things I wanted to organize, but never could, was an international conference on Black voting rights to look at how people around the world, but particularly in Western Europe, the United States, and Canada, are experiencing voting rights. What can we learn? What can we share? What seems to work? What seems to not work?

So there are a number of concrete steps that we can take that bring African Americans in direct connection with people who are doing similar efforts over in Europe. And in that way we begin to institutionalize our relationships, and we begin to have ongoing, long-term kinds of relationships that can turn into projects and turn into concrete changes.

Mr. SMITH. We are joined by the distinguished chairman of the Africa Subcommittee, the Africa Global Health Subcommittee of the Foreign Affairs Committee, Donald Payne, my good friend from New Jersey.

HON. DONALD M. PAYNE (D–10) A MEMBER OF CONGRESS FROM THE STATE OF NEW JERSEY

Mr. PAYNE. It's really a pleasure to be here, and I really enjoyed the little bit that I've heard. My plane was delayed coming down, and so I apologize.

Nice to see you again in the United States, Dr. Lusane. The last time I think I saw you was in the Netherlands.

However, I've listened with interest, and I think that it's really appropriate that we start to raise the issue of people of color in Europe. When you look at the fact that colonization was a part of the European experience and the exploitation that Europe did varied with different colonial powers and others—I guess Belgium was the worst—but all of them were degrading in many instances.

As a result, we see many states that are still grappling in Africa, for example, to have some governance and it's the legacy, I think, of slavers.

As a matter of fact, we created and passed a bill to create a commission on the bicentennial abolition of the slave trade, which occurred in the United States in 1908, voted into law in 1807 and signed by President Jefferson, I think, in 1808, became law a year after Britain did it under the leadership of Mr. Wilberforce.

They had a year-long celebration in Britain, where they studied the impact of transatlantic slavery. I think they had all kinds of foundations—it might have been as much as $100 million—that went to schools, where they had a total discussion of the impact of transatlantic slavery and what it had.

I'm hoping that our Commission will be able to do the same thing. We've been unable to get funding, but we're going to still struggle to see if we can at least match Great Britain—just Britain now.

I do believe that with the different phases of Europe, at one time African Americans felt it was the place to go—to France—the entertainers, and they saw less discrimination. I think maybe when numbers grow, then perhaps things change, because that was back when Josephine Baker and Ray Robinson, the boxer, and those people were going to France in particular.

Europe tended to embrace people of color more so during the time of a lot of discrimination in the United States. It appears, though, that things may be changing. Of course, a lot of, I think, racism started at World War II when White soldiers portrayed Black soldiers as different and started stereotypes during World War II.

That was an area that I spent a lot of time studying. My uncle was in the invasion of Normandy on D-Day, and so his experiences there were kind of interesting to me as a young boy, hearing him talk about what happened there.

I do think that there is some affirmative action that is going on, of course, in Northern Ireland—not between races, but with the McBride principles that say you have to hire a Catholic anytime you hire a Protestant, if they're doing business with the United States.

There are the new policing laws in Belfast in the north of Ireland, where there's a quota. You can't hire a Protestant policeman until you hire a Catholic policeman, because in Northern Ireland 98 percent of the police department were Protestants, and 98 percent of the prisoners were Catholics, and so they felt there might be a little something wrong with that formula.

So affirmative action is really in play in Northern Ireland, like I said, on the religious front. So these are really some issues that may be brought into Europe as we focus more on the question.

In Latin America there was a lot of attention in 2002. The Afro Latinos came to the Congressional Black Caucus and started to tell us about the plight of African descendants in the Americas and we kind of created a working group. And as a result, there have been a lot of activity and changes in Brazil. They've moved forward with trying to have a strong affirmative action program.

In Colombia President Uribe has come to my office several times and has made cabinet level positions and even in the government focusing on even in higher education. In Peru they're looking at the whole question—even in Mexico, Mexicans of African descent.

Of course, they have a long way to go, but there is now a realization that there needs to be some kind of affirmative action on the part to discuss the legacy of discrimination in their countries.

I do recall when they had a Congressional Black Caucus in Britain. I visited them in '95 and spoke in several cities with the president or chairman of the Black Caucus. It was a mixture of Indian and Blacks.

At that time we were dealing with the British police's choke hold where in prison there were a number of deaths by the manner in which the British police would restrain—and not even restrain, but just it was a practice—and there were a number of deaths, all of minorities, that died with the choke hold and we had discussions on that.

I guess my question is do you think that some similar kind of group as we have in Latin America—of course, I think that Latin America probably is very much behind Europe; it definitely was the treatment of African descendants in Latin America in general in the Americas, I believe was much worse than that in Europe—but do you think that some similar kind of attention or thrust would be appropriate at this time?

Dr. LUSANE. Yes. I think that's an excellent idea. There are a number of groups in Europe: from the Black Germany Initiative, which is in Germany; ADEFRA, which is a Black German women's organization; Diaspora Afrique, which is based in Paris; POMOSIA, which is based in Austria; SOS Racism, which is based in Spain and a couple of other countries.

There are a large number of organizations that would be happy and more than willing to engage in the kind of dialogue that happened with the Afro Latino experiences. I think if we can move along those lines, that would be a major step forward.

Mr. PAYNE. Great.

Dr. ESSED. Yes, I agree with that. I also agree that it would be very good to learn from Brazil, for instance, where they have progressive anti-discrimination laws which, from what I hear, are also being implemented with some rigor.

Dr. BLAKELY. I do think there are a growing number of resources in Europe. In the academic world, for example, there are more and more centers being established that are dealing with these issues. So if there were such a group, they wouldn't have to be starting from scratch in terms of trying to find out what's going on.

Mr. PAYNE. Well, you know, that's a great idea. As a matter of fact, about 5 years ago I was invited to speak at the NAACP branch in Germany. It was interesting. It was founded by some American Black that moved to Germany 25 years ago, and they have an NAACP chapter, and I found it very interesting.

There will be a followup to the Durban conference on racism and xenophobia and so forth. Of course, we may recall that the first conference became hijacked, more or less, by an issue of the Palestinians and Israel—and it diverted the whole intent of the convention, which was to deal with racism in the world.

It was unfortunate that a group of radicals destroyed the opportunity, really, for a legitimate discussion and debate on what the conference was really supposed to primarily focus on—on racism.

I'm hoping that the followup to Durban could have the full participation of all the countries, but somehow box that or eliminate the hijacking of this very important convention, because I think the people of African descent all around the world suffered because of some extremist anti-Israeli proponents that hijacked this conference and made it about what it wasn't supposed to be about.

So I am hoping that can be eliminated, so this whole question of racism around the world—because Durban is the only forum that's ever been created for this, and unfortunately it was tarnished and actually not fully participated in, especially by the United States and other countries, so I don't know if any of you all are going to participate in the Durban II, but that would be a forum, I think, that if it's done properly, could really be a real sounding board. It's going to be scheduled for 2009, although preparatory meetings are being held in Geneva, as we speak, as a matter of fact.

Dr. LUSANE. I would agree with you. I think it was very unfortunate circumstances that ultimately occurred.

At the regional level, things were much better. I was working in Europe at the time and helped the work on the European regional preparatory conference for Durban, and that was really an opportunity for bringing together groups who were working on racism, immigration issues, anti-Semitism, kind of across the board.

That process hopefully will be emerged around 2009 and particularly focused on the national action plans that were agreed upon by most member states that attended the conference.

There has been some followup, but it's wilted a little bit, and so the process of heading toward 2009, hopefully, at least at the European level, will re-ignite the energy around pushing some of the states, and particularly some of the new states that have come into the EU, to followup either on the national action plans they agreed to, or something along those lines around policy dealing with anti-discrimination and anti-racism.

Mr. PAYNE. Just a last question. I know that in the athletic realm with the soccer or their football, I guess, as you call it there, that there have been more and more stars of African descent and from what I understand, there have been sort of racial attacks by fans.

Of course, it seems—I don't want to prejudge any group—but seems like kind of hooligans kind of follow those big games and it seems that drinking and all of that becomes as much a part of the game, and so before the game is over, I don't even know if anyone's really watching the game or they're just out fighting or brawling.

At one time one country barred another country from coming to the game. It's just gotten out of control.

But as relates to Black soccer stars and the name-calling that occurs, has that been a problem more at the side, or was it an issue?

Dr. BLAKELY. It's still very much an issue. Within the last year, there have been really horrible incidents reported in the press. For example, there was incident in Germany where a Nigerian soccer star was taunted by fans, and bananas were thrown, and he became so upset that he raised a Hitler salute.

It turns out this against the law in Germany, so he was brought up on charges. Nothing was done to the fans. And that sort of says where things are, except there have recently been measures taken by a couple of countries to crack down on that kind of violence.

As you know, law enforcement doesn't necessarily change hearts and it's still a tradition in some countries. It's sort of been, in varying levels of intensity—they thought they'd gotten control of it by the 80s, but then there was another upsurge again with the ultranationalists and the skinheads and so.

So the jury is still out, whether or not that's going to be held completely in check.

Dr. LUSANE. What I would add to that, though, is that coming out of the 80s and 90s, there are actually some excellent policies that are in place in a couple of countries, like the U.K., for example, working with the football teams, working with local jurisdictions. They have put in some models of how to address the issues.

And there are some organizations, like Keep Racism Out of Football, that also exist. What doesn't exist is at the European level and leadership from the E.U. on this particular issue that would begin to propose a directive or something that would give some strength to what are fairly good policies that exist in a couple of countries but in other countries, as Dr. Blakely said, there's virtually nothing solved.

Mr. PAYNE. Thank you very much.

Thank you, Mr. Chairman.

Mr. SMITH. Thank you.

Just very briefly, if you could tell us what countries you think are the best in Europe in terms of combating racism? And second, has the European Court of Human Rights been used with any effectiveness by people whose rights have been infringed upon?

Dr. LUSANE. In terms of the first question——

Mr. SMITH. You might add what countries are the worst.

Dr. LUSANE. Oh, there are a lot of worst countries. But in terms of countries that are doing best, in terms of overall framework, I would say the U.K. and the Netherlands.

What they have put in place, particularly in the U.K. as a result of the Race Relations Amendment Act in 2000, is that it not only addresses anti-discrimination, but equality.

For example, all public bodies—and there are over 40,000 in the U.K., from local councils to local health care centers—are all required to do an analysis of their policies to see how those policies impact on race relations.

So there are some advanced kinds of thinking that went on in public places similarly in the Netherlands but in a number of places, you simply have nothing that approaches that at all.

The second question was——

Mr. SMITH. The European Court of Human Rights.

Dr. LUSANE [continuing]. The European Court of Human Rights. The big problem with the European Court of Human Rights is that under the European Convention, Article 14, which is the article that specifically deals with discrimination, is not a stand-alone article and it can only be invoked in association with another violation under the Convention.

There is a protocol that has been proposed, for now probably 8 or 9 years, that would resolve the issue, but only a few states have signed on to it.

The European Court of Human Rights can actually be a very positive environment and a number of rulings from the court have had a reverberating impact across the region and so it takes quite a while to get a case through, but when the cases do go through, they impact on all the member states, because all 43 countries larger than the E.U. are members of the Council of Europe.

So it can be an instrument, but right now the major problem is getting Article 14 to be a stand-alone and pushing for Protocol 12 to be passed.

Dr. ESSED. I want to qualify which country you take as an example. I would say in the U.K. the combination of well organized and long time community resistance has been very important and the U.K. is advanced in that.

As for the Netherlands, anti-discrimination policies are fairly well in place, but the Netherlands has the highest degree of exclusions from the labor market. Take that as a measure and they end up at the bottom.

I continue to emphasize, it's important to look at what actually happens on a day-to-day basis and not to be fooled blinded by progressive policies or nice words only.

Mr. PAYNE. Would you yield?

Mr. SMITH. Yes.

Mr. PAYNE. Ireland has been the country that is the new engine of Europe—the E.U., when they came in with their plan of upgrading the south of Europe to fix bridges and roads and so forth, and somehow Ireland caught on fire. They were maybe 10 millionaires 20 years ago, but now there are several hundred—just almost the highest per capita income.

However, I understand that it is more difficult in Ireland for a person of African descent to even get an appointment at the Irish Embassy that would handle that.

Have you or anyone looked at what's happening in Ireland and how strong the racial discrimination, with all the battle between sectarianism and trying to resolve Northern Ireland—of course, that's another country—but Catholics and Protestants and knowing what all the problems were for Ireland?

I've spoken to some of the Sinn Fein people, former IRA folks, who are very disappointed. They're in the north of Ireland, very disappointed in what is happening in Ireland.

They just can't believe that racial discrimination would happen, because they went through so much religious discrimination in the north of Ireland, and they're just so displeased with the government of Ireland. I mean, even today we're going to have the Taoiseach who's going to address the Congress, I think, today.

Has anyone studied or know specifically about the Irish experience that's going on right now?

Dr. BLAKELY. I have, in fact, been giving special attention to Ireland, in part because the recent influx of African population has been so sudden—about 30,000, seemingly, over less than a decade—and apace with that, unfortunately, has been the rise of discrimination.

There have been a couple of Black elected officials, though, even along with that. It's difficult to say exactly which way things are going right now, because things are in flux. But they're at least aware in Ireland that there is a problem, and I think they are trying to move to address it.

That would also determine my ranking of how the other countries are doing. I think those who acknowledge that there is a problem are way ahead of the game and that's why I do place England and the Netherlands on the top in that respect.

The ones who are still denying that they want to deal with those kinds of categories, I think, are not going to move toward any resolutions of the very real problems. So I think that that's really the main factor. It's an attitudinal question about are you going to address these issues or not.

One other country I would mention with respect to that, another country with a sizable population, about half a million, is Italy, which actually looks pretty bright, although there are problems there but, again, attitudinally I think there was a conscious decision by the Italian authorities that they're going to avoid some of these problems that are happening elsewhere.

There is also the historical tradition there and the proximity to Africa and other kinds of factors that play a role in this.

Mr. PAYNE. Right. Just reclaiming for a second, I think you're absolutely right, and I think that in Ethiopia and Italy there's been a long kind of relationship—many times adverse.

The thing about Ireland is that it's so new. Ireland has been a country that has had a net loss for 150 years. No one ever went to Ireland. They all left Ireland, as you know, from the 1848 potato famine all through the years, because the economics were so bleak.

Now it has turned around, where you are starting to have a big net increase. As a matter of fact, Irish Americans, came on home. You'll get a better deal over here than you've got over there.

But I think that the newness of this immigration that they're confronted with now, with the economics just off the charts, is something that I think might be more than they can even come up to grips with.

I hope that they take advantage of countries like Britain or others—the one that you say is the best—to follow what they've done to try to avoid really being caught up in something that's 20, 30 years ago that other countries have dealt with.

Mr. SMITH. I want to thank you for your testimonies, for your incisive answers to questions posed by the panel and there may be some additional questions. If you could get back in a timely fashion to us, that would be greatly appreciated, so it could become part of the record.

But thank you again.

The hearing is adjourned.

[Whereupon, at 12:21 p.m., the hearing was adjourned.]

APPENDICES

PREPARED STATEMENT OF HON. ALCEE L. HASTINGS, CHAIRMAN, COMMISSION ON SECURITY AND COOPERATION IN EUROPE

Good morning, ladies and gentleman. Thank you for your interest in this morning's hearing focussed on the experiences of Blacks in Europe. For many years, I have travelled to Europe as a tourist, Member of Congress, President of the OSCE Parliamentary Assembly, and now as Chairman of the Helsinki Commission.

On those trips, I would often meet other Black people living or travelling in Europe, who were thrilled to meet another Black person. This was especially true when I was travelling in the former Soviet Union.

Not always so thrilling were the stories they would share with me of the racism they faced. Worse, I, too, was the victim of racial profiling by authorities and blatant discrimination, such as when I was refused service at European establishments.

In this regard, there are a number of similarities between my experiences as a Black American and those of Black Europeans. So one central goal of this hearing is to highlight and address the very real problems of racism and discrimination faced by Black Europeans.

Another goal is to also recall the contributions Blacks have made to Europe and the world by removing the cloak of invisibility that for so long has served as a shroud.

Recognizing and demythologizing the roles of Blacks in European history and modern day society has become a necessity given the rise of virulent anti-immigrant campaigns that target non-Whites in the aftermath of 9/11 and the London bombings. Whether Blacks were forced or chose to assist in Europe's development, they did play a role that should be noted.

As globalization continues to bring the world closer together, how European countries choose to define themselves and their peoples affects us all and will most certainly affect how I am viewed and treated at and within Europe's borders.

A third goal of this hearing is to then develop partnerships with those overseas committed to addressing these problems. Too often we highlight the problems within countries without noting the efforts that are being made—be they government, civil society, or even the private sector. The OSCE's High Commissioner on National Minorities as well as the EU Fundamental Rights Agency have compiled reports on European countries' positive initiatives ranging from affirmative action to housing and education desegregation.

These are all efforts that have already been tried in the U.S. We need to be asking ourselves, how can we best extend a helping hand so that Europeans don't repeat some of the mistakes we made here in developing and implementing these programs?

A fourth point, which requires us to be honest with ourselves—is that there are a number of very real barriers to addressing inclusion goals for Black Europeans ranging from the small size of some communities to a need for differences in approach for recent migrant versus more established communities.

I am glad to have such esteemed witnesses here today to present thoughts on all of these issues. I would therefore like to introduce Mr. Frans joining us from Sweden and Mr. Younge joining us from the UK via New York to speak about their work.

Unfortunately, due to scheduling constraints around Mr. Kodjoe's role in the Broadway play "Cat on a Hot Tin Roof," he is unable to be here today. He has however indicated his support for this and future initiatives on Blacks in Europe and asked that I enter his statement in the record. Which I hereby do. I would also at this time like to enter the statements of some of our European friends, the Initiative of Black Germans, Diaspora Afrique, and the Black European Women's Congress.

Now, because the issue of Afro-descendants in Europe touches on so many aspects of the Helsinki Commission's work—human rights, security, migration—I am also planning to introduce legislation recognizing Black Europeans and calling for initiatives within the OSCE to address their plight. Your thoughts here today will be central to those efforts.

I would also like to thank my fellow Commissioners for being here and would welcome your remarks at this time.

PREPARED STATEMENT OF HON. BENJAMIN L. CARDIN, CO-CHAIRMAN, COMMISSION ON SECURITY AND COOPERATION IN EUROPE

As we commemorate the 200th Anniversary of the abolition of the Transatlantic Slave Trade and the 40th Anniversary of the death of Martin Luther King Jr. this year it is only right that we take a closer look at the state of race relations in this country, as well as determine where other countries are in their commitment to uphold and respect fundamental freedoms and rights without distinction.

The nooses of Jena, Louisiana and, indeed, in my own State of Maryland, tell us that despite the sacrifices of Dr. Martin Luther King Jr. and untold others, we still have much work to do on in this country. It is for this reason that I introduced legislation in the Senate calling for the full investigation and criminal prosecution of the hanging of nooses and will continue efforts to fight racism and its effects in our society.

However, we must also note that the bigotry we have seen in the United States is not a unique phenomenon limited to the confines of our own borders. The OSCE, Russia's SOVA Center, Union of Councils for Soviet Jews, and Human Rights First have all recorded increases in racist murders and other hate crimes in Russia and Ukraine. For the past few years, the European Union Federal Rights Agency has recorded more than 80,000 racist incidents and over 17,000 crimes linked to hate groups annually in the European Union.

Hate crimes. Racial profiling. Rampant discrimination in employment, education, housing, and other sectors are disproportionately impacting African descendants and other minorities. The French riots alerted us to the gross disparities between those living in France's suburbs, similar to the urban ghettos of the US, and the rest of France's population. Chants of monkey noises amidst a hail of bananas raining down on soccer fields brought to the world's attention the racism targeting Black soccer players in Europe.

When paired with the racist, xenophobic, and anti-immigrant remarks of some of Europe's politicians, it is not difficult to understand how some Europeans might believe such behavior is not only sanctioned, but a part of their civic duty to push out those that don't fit their image of Europe. Our own immigration debates, recent efforts to erode the gains of the Civil Rights struggle, and attempts to relegate racism as a thing of this countries' past despite persistent disparities, demonstrate a need for comprehensive strategies and partnerships to combat hate and its ramifications.

Don't get me wrong, President Putin's admission that racism is a problem in Russia, the Ukrainian creation of a special security unit to combat xenophobia, and President Sarkozy's new government plan for France's poor communities, are all steps in the right direction, but not enough. The hard truth is we all need to be doing more, including holding one another accountable. By learning from one another and developing sustainable partnerships, we can.

We, as Americans, must share what we have learned to become a multi-racial society so that others need not repeat our mistakes. We also must support increased interactions between European minorities and US based civil rights organizations, assistance for European governments in their efforts to combat discrimination, and parliamentary initiatives to combat hateful party politics. To paraphrase the slogan to address racism in soccer, we must kick racism and its ramifications out of our societies.

I look forward to hearing our witnesses' thoughts on what more we can all be doing to promote diversity and understanding while combating hate in all of our societies.

Thank you.

PREPARED STATEMENT OF HON. G.K. BUTTERFIELD, COMMISSIONER, COMMISSION ON SECURITY AND COOPERATION IN EUROPE

Thank you, Mr. Chairman, for holding this very important hearing. As the son of an immigrant from a former British colony, I have been touched by both the colonial and migrant experience. Both issues are of great relevance for this hearing, as they are related to some of the often overlooked roles blacks have played in Europe's development.

My father was from Bermuda, now the oldest self-governing overseas territory in the British Commonwealth. A British colony formed in the 1600s, Bermuda's economy was based on the islands' cedar trees for shipbuilding and the salt trade and sustained by African slave labor. With the slave trade outlawed in Bermuda in 1807, and slaves freed in 1834, today over 60% of Bermudians are of African descent.

A number of Bermudians have migrated to the British mainland. However long before their migration, they and their forbearers assisted in the building of Europe's economy and made countless other contributions to Europe's social fabric.

History is not so different for those in the Caribbean countries of Suriname and Curacao who migrated from their former colonies to the Netherlands; Haiti and Senegal who migrated to France; and the numerous other examples that could be cited with a number of these migration patterns from the Caribbean and Africa continuing until today.

Despite these truths, the ills of slavery and its repercussions have often been a distinction solely reserved for the U.S. and its black population. Recent efforts in the UN and Europe commemorating the 200th Anniversary of the abolition of the transatlantic slave trade have assisted in raising the visibility of and recalling these histories.

The UK constructed a replica of the Amistad, the 19th century ship to retrace a 14,000-mile slave route, including stops in the US, Africa, Caribbean and UK. A BBC website noting the impact colonialism and slavery has had on how Blacks are viewed and perceived in the world has also been erected. Athletic prowess, exoticism and low intelligence were all stereotypes used to justify slavery and colonialism, and still exist today. These stereotypes impact how we are portrayed in the global media, our education and employment opportunities, and why many of our contributions have remained invisible to the world.

To recognize us means challenging European notions of being mono-racial and mono-cultural nations. To recognize us means that far-right parties calling to keep Europe "European" have no grounds, for we are also part of Europe.

Today, we are being recognized. Mr. Chairman, I thank you for this and look forward to hearing from our witnesses on how best we can all work together to promote diverse societies that extend and protect fundamental rights to everyone.

Thank you.

PREPARED STATEMENT OF JOE FRANS, VICE CHAIR, UNITED NATIONS WORKING GROUP ON PEOPLE OF AFRICAN DESCENT, AND FORMER SWEDISH PARLIAMENTARIAN

Chairman Hastings, Ladies and Gentlemen, It gives me great pleasure and honour to be here with you here today. I am pleased that you have chosen the topic of the African Diaspora in Europe for this particular hearing. It is a timely intervention and a most relevant one. This is simply because Europe is currently undergoing a soul searching experience of its own identity.

I would like to begin this brief presentation by paying tribute to the millions of African people abducted and enslaved and to those who sacrificed their lives in fighting for national liberation in Africa and in the Diaspora. They have inspired our thinking and indeed generated our current desire to contribute as a Diaspora to the development of Africa.

The African Diaspora consists of peoples of African origin living outside the continent, irrespective of their citizenship and nationality and who are willing to contribute to the development of the continent and the building of the Africa. Today, there are over 3.3 million people of African descent living in Europe according to Eurostat. Over 1 million are from sub-Saharan Africa.

In the post WWII era, the need for cheap labor to rebuild Europe resulted in inflows of Africans to Europe. The post-independence era further generated an inflow of African students. Political conflicts in Africa itself, the cold war and related global competition for economic development has also generated an inflow of asylum seekers and refugees. In addition, there has been a steady stream of African-European families who have chosen to settle in Europe as a matter of choice.

Today, besides the above reasons, the benefits of the trickle of migrants is double-sided. On the one hand, the reserve of cheap labor—often described as unwanted—is used as a regulator, as seen in the flow of migrants across the Mediterranean in scranky boats with life itself at stake and who try to reach Europe by literally swimming the last mile. On the other hand, the question of whether attracting and sourcing highly skilled migrants from Africa to Europe are needed to sustain gains for Africa must be raised. Basically, African countries are funding the education of their nationals only to see them contributing to the growth of developed countries with seemingly little or no return on their investment. And yet, at closer look, Africans are contributing to the development of European identity and of the African continent itself. Some estimates suggest that Africans working abroad send home some US$45 billion a year. This is bigger than the total development aid and bigger than the total foreign direct investment.

However, the challenges of integrating this new workforce remain. At the concluding session of the European Conference against Racism in 2000, a Political Declaration was adopted by Ministers of the Council of Europe Member States. In the document, the Governments concluded that the continued and violent occurrence of racism is an issue of concern and that challenges of integrating young people, immigrants and other groups remain, especially in the labor market where discrimination is present. A report presented by the British Trade Unions (TUC) Congress, argues that at every level of working life many black workers are being denied training opportunities—despite often being better qualified than their white counterparts. Discriminatory practices at work are still preventing too many workers in Europe with African descent from fulfilling their potential.

However, statistics in the public domain to support arguments of racial violence and workplace discrimination in Western Europe are embarrassingly lacking. Without official statistics, effective responses cannot be devised. One of the most common indicators of labor market inequality is the rate of unemployment for immigrants and/or minorities. In 2005, it was reported that the unemployment rates for such groups were all significantly higher than for the majority population in many European countries. It is quite clear that thousands of people of African descent live in miserable conditions. Those without legal documents have no access to the welfare state, are exploited as cheap labor, and have no rights.

Quite clearly, racism and discrimination are relevant to understanding the commonality of challenges of people of African descent in Western Europe.

And yet there are also positive stories. All countries have constitutional frameworks against discrimination. There are many success stories in politics, policy dialogue, business and education, yet I have chosen to focus on those issues that demand our attention in framing policy.

Mr. Chairman, one policy idea that could benefit from your support is the promotion of a trans-Atlantic dialogue on the experiences of people of African Descent. I would welcome both your support and assistance in making this happen. Thank you.

PREPARED STATEMENT OF GARY YOUNGE, BRITISH COLUMNIST, THE GUARDIAN NEWSPAPER

My mother came to London from Barbados in the early 60s with a British passport and two A-levels in European history and English literature. She could quote from A Winter's Tale, but knew only heat and hurricane. Before she left the island she was given orientation classes to prepare her for life in Britain. They told her to wear flannelette pyjamas and a woollen hat. They said nothing about people shouting abuse at you in the street.

She came of her own free will. She also came because she was asked by the British government to help to build one of the nation's most cherished institutions, the National Health Service. Racism and the cold aside, two of the things to strike her when she arrived were that most British people seemed to know very little about their own country, and even less about the nations their country had occupied. In the words of Gilbert, a Jamaican immigrant in Andrea Levy's award-winning novel Small Island. "But for me I had just one question—let me ask the Mother Country just this one simple question: how come England did not know me?"

These elements of my mother's story will form the basis of my testimony today, drawing as they do on some of the central threads of the black European experience versus the American experience. Europe did have a civil rights movement. It took place at roughly the same time as the US civil rights movement and around the same issues—the right to vote, opposition to segregation and a more equal share of resources. But it did not take place in Europe. For the most part it primarily took place abroad—in Algeria, Ghana, India, Mozambique, Congo etc. That has left a local indigenous population in Europe with little understanding of or sense of historical responsibility to those whom it once colonized.

The screams of the oppressed tortured by colonialism were uttered continents away and were neither heard at home. So there has been little in the way of moral reckoning with our past. But when it comes to domestic matters there is little in the way of historical literacy that would explain either European power or the presence of non-white people in Europe. In the words of the venerable director of the Institute of Race Relations in Britain, Ambalavaner Sivanandan: "We are here because you were there." But if you didn't know you were there, how could you understand why we are here?

This ignorance can and has lead to severe racial antagonism which over the past 20 years has reinstalled itself as a permanent fixture in European political culture. Fascism—or at least the xenophobic, racist and nationalistic elements that are its most vile manifestations—has returned as a mainstream ideology in Europe. Its advocates not only run in elections but win them. They control local councils and sit in parliaments.

In Austria, Belgium, Denmark, France and Italy, hard-right nationalist and anti-immigrant parties regularly receive more than 10 percent of the vote. In Norway it is 22 percent; in Switzerland, 29 percent. In Austria they have been in government; in Switzerland, where the anti-immigrant Swiss People's Party is the largest party, they still are. In Italy they are about to return to government again. A central plank of these parties' platforms rests on the notion that each nation is a mono-racial and cultural unit into which non-white people have come and must on entry either conform or be banished. This or course is hinged on an entirely mythical notion of white European uniformity which must be defended against the uncivilized and the unwashed.

Conversely on the level of daily cultural interaction it is difficult to imagine the continent without non-white people. In literature, music, sport we have become so inextricably intertwined in the national fabric that to unpick us would make that whole cloth unravel. But that has not stopped many from trying.

Particularly since September 11th the push to assimilate into a society that won't house, educate, employ or even respect you has become particularly intense. Like many my mother who took a low-paid steady job—the industries that non -white people went into depend largely on the countries they went to and came from. But the industries and sectors our parents went into have for the most part shrunk or been decimated leaving relatively limited opportunities for their children.

In Europe there is no black middle class. There are black middle class individuals. But no class as such. For their children the dislocation between our race—our colour—and place—where you are, appears at times unshakeable. Those who have been in France or Germany for generations are still called immigrants. And on that note, I will end with the conversation I had with an old man while I was at university in Edinburgh who asked me where I was from. "Stevenage," I said. "Where were you born?" "Hitchin," I said. "Well, before then." "Well, there was no before then." "Well, where are you're parents from," "Barbados." "Ahh, you're from Barbados." "No, I'm from Stevenage."

PREPARED STATEMENT OF PHILOMENA ESSED, ANTIOCH UNIVERSITY, THE NETHERLANDS, EQUAL TREATMENT COMMISSION

Thank you for inviting me to this hearing on people of Afro-descent in Europe. By way of introduction I will present an alphabetical list of key concepts and notions relevant to understanding social conditions and experiences of Afro-descendants in Europe. It is not my intention to pretend completeness, but to provide a hopefully practical approach to a complex theme.

AFRO-EUROPEAN

Afro-European, as a possible equivalent to the notion of African-American, does not exist in any legal, social or practical sense. In Europe, European and brown/black skin color are perceived as mutually exclusive categories. Afro-descendant immigrants do not merge or integrate into any broader category or community of 'Afro-Europeans'. Afro- refers to a variety of communities and individuals, originating from different continents and countries, speaking different mother tongues and/or different European languages according to the country in which they reside.

The (historical) relation to specific European countries forms another variant. The majority are the descendants of colonized people (Africa, South America). This group includes the descendants of enslaved Africans in the (former) European colonies (The Caribbean, South America). Many came to Europe as workers (North and sub-Sahara Africa; the Caribbean; South America) in search for a better future. There are individuals who migrated as students in the context of development cooperation (African students to former communist countries). There are political and economic refugees (including (Ethiopia, Eritrea, Somalia, and other war conflicted areas) who have settled in a range of European countries.

An increasing number of people of Afro-descent are born in Europe from parents who immigrated to Europe, or from Afro-descendants and white partners. In addition, African children have been adopted into European families. Some people of Afro-descent live in communities of national/ethnic origin while others have been assimilated into white communities. A case in point are Afro-Germans, often the children of white German women and African (former) students (East Germany) or African American soldiers, many of whom grew up with their mothers. They are culturally German and racially Black. There are significant numbers of culturally assimilated middles class Afro-descendants. But Afro-descendants are also overrepresented among the European poor. Depending on the context or their lives, conditions of arrival and national backgrounds, different needs and goals may be the focus of their struggles: citizenship, illegality, language acquisition, religious rights, economics, dealing with traumas of war, homelessness, unemployment, or glass ceilings.

To label individuals and groups who are as heterogeneous and unconnected as the above with the one label of 'Afro-descendants' is not uncontroversial. Many share only (some) phenotypical, or if you wish, racial resemblances. Probably the only common European experience among many if not all Afro-descendants is their exposure to (a certain degree of) racism and systemic discrimination, regardless of country, socio-economic conditions, gender, age, or level of education.

BLACK EUROPEAN

Different than in the US, Black as a notion is not exclusively used to refer to people of African descent. In particular among critical scholars and community activists the indication of 'Black' has been applied indiscriminately to targets of discrimination on the basis of race, culture, ethnicity, religion or a combination of these factors. This inclusive interpretation has been contested by Asians who do not want to be seen as 'Black', or by Afro-descendants who protest against the cooptation of 'their' identity as 'Black'. In the new millennium a cross-European movement has emerged claiming 'Black European' as their experience and identity. This diverse group of people tends to be more inclusive of others than 'Afro-descendants, but the last word has certainly not been said about the question of 'Who is Black?'

COLONIALISM

For many people of Afro-descent, the historical contexts of reference are colonialism and post-colonialism rather than slavery, even when they might be descendants of enslaved Africans (Caribbean, South American backgrounds). Many came to the so-called motherlands in Europe with European passports (for instance, immigrants from Surinamese and the Dutch Antilles to the Netherlands, French immigrants from Martinique to France). Colonialism, its economical, social and psychological implications and consequences are largely ignored in the European canons.

Colonial relations continue to exist, including the inequalities involved. The Dutch Antillean colonies, for instance, are a popular tourist attraction for (white) Dutch. For the local population the reality is different. Extremely high unemployment numbers in the Dutch Antilles, unrealistic ideas about 'rich lives' in the Netherlands, or the desire to reunite with emigrated family, have caused high numbers to migrate to the Netherlands. Insufficient care, social indifference, lack of schooling and job opportunities, racial prejudice and a sense of anonymity in the Netherlands contribute to violence and criminality among young Antillean men. In response, the state seems to entertain controversial (and probably unlawful) ethnic databases on Antilleans, on the basis of which enhanced security and preventive law enforcement interventions can take place. Among Antillean women teenage pregnancies are a problem, often the result of a combination of factors, including physical or emotional abandonment at home, racial discrimination, and ignorance.

The consequences of colonialism have not been dealt with in Europe. This holds true for the dependency mentality (passivity and sense of powerlessness among formerly colonized) as well as for the remnants of the European colonial mentality (paternalism and the creation of second class citizens).

Denial of racism

In the course of the 1990s racial discrimination has been placed on the agenda of European Union members. But in most policy and public discourse the application of the word racism has not moved beyond the 1950's model of explicit race hierarchies (exceptions are a number of critical scholars and antiracism activists). Since many European countries reject the idea of race hierarchies on moral grounds, it is assumed that that 'therefore' there is no racism. In this view racism is an aberration of a few extremist groups only. The many subtle and cultural forms it takes (sense of European cultural superiority) are ignored. When it comes to accountability, each and every member state looks the other way: racism might be out there, but never here, not in their specific country. A frequently used, but misleading argument is that racism is an American thing.

Everyday racism

Racism is integrated in the routine practices of everyday European cultures and institutions resulting in informally segregated neighborhoods (UK, France, Germany), formally sanctioned segregated schools, so called Black and White schools (the Netherlands), neighborhood harassment of refugee families (for instance Spain, or the recent case of a Liberian family in the Netherlands); police violence (for instance in Austria), and so on. Among the most damaging forms of everyday racism are those involving individuals in positions of authority, whose decision-making power has the potential of making or breaking study careers or professional opportunities. Due to the public taboo on mentioning racism and emotional if not aggressive response to accusations of racism from the side of white Europeans, many Afro-descendants are neither aware of racism, nor sufficiently equipped to resist. Frequently, those exposed to racism experience a sense of powerlessness in the face of accusations that they are 'just oversensitive'.

Systemic exposure to racial discrimination is stressful, which can take a toll on the (mental) health of victims. Whether or not directly related, there are indications in the UK and in the Netherlands that disproportionate numbers of people of Afro-descent are diagnosed with schizophrenia. It remains unclear whether this is a result of misdiagnosis, an increase in mental health problems, or an increase in the number of people of Afro-decent people visiting mental health clinics.

The impact of everyday racism on the lives of black and brown people continues to be a neglected issue among European policy makers.

Fortress Europe

Increasingly tight borders since the Schengen Treaty are not preventing economic and war refugees from risking their lives in search of a better future in Europe. Many die prematurely in the passage between North Africa and Southern Europe: young men, women, and children. In the meantime middlemen are making blood money. The construction of 'illegality' has different impacts on men and women. Little is known about the particular conditions of illegal immigrants who try to survive as street vendors (mostly male, mostly in southern Europe), domestics (mostly women), or in prostitution (mostly women, but also including young Moroccan men).

GENDER

Race is not gender neutral. Perceptions of Afro-descendants, men and women, are shaped by many factors, including histories of colonialism (white males, native mistresses); imagined exoticism (female warmth, sensuality and active sexuality) recurrent media images of African wars and poverty (male aggression) and African-American images through the media (sports, music).

The sex trade and abuse of African women have been reported, among others in Belgium. In the Netherlands, where prostitution is legal, women of Afro-descent end up in the lowest paid and most risky sectors of sex work. Beauty norms are another gender issue. Little is known in Europe about the impact of white beauty norms on women of Afro descent. Skin bleaching has been found to be a problem among women of Ghanaian background in the Netherlands. Circumcision of girls occurs, for instance, among refugees from Somalia. Policy makers have not been successful in including the women of these communities in endeavors to put an end to this practice.

In schools Afro-descendant girls from Caribbean origin families are outperforming male counterparts in the Netherlands. The percentage of highly educated women among Afro-descendant women from the Caribbean is more or less equal to that of highly educated white Dutch women. This does not translate into equal representation at higher levels of the labor market.

HISTORY

The historical relation between Africa and Europe is hardly an area of interest in school curricula. The historical presence of Africa in Europe has been the object of study among a few experts, but it is certainly not part of common sense knowledge among populations in Europe, and far from being considered a constitutive part of European history proper.

IDENTITY

Even when they can be formally categorized as a person of Afro-descent, not all individuals and groups identify with 'color' or 'race'. Many identify foremost in terms of their country of origin. It should also be noted that in the cosmopolitan cities such as Paris, London, Amsterdam there is an increasing African American presence (students, immigrants, tourists).

JEWS

Very little is known about Afro-Jews in Europe, including, for instance, mixed race descendants from the (former) Dutch colonies of Suriname and the Dutch Antilles. There is reason for concern about sections among (North African) Muslims whose critique of

Israeli state politics often is considered to transform into anti-Semitism against Jews in Europe.

KKK

Europe does not have a KKK, but neo-Nazi and white supremacist groups are active.

Laws

The European anti-discrimination laws of the 1990s have been important in creating procedures to deal with discrimination in organizational contexts. Different European countries have organized their own government funded, independent antidiscrimination agencies. In the Netherlands there is the Dutch Equal Treatment Commission the mission of which is to promote, monitor, and advise on compliance with the Dutch equal treatment legislation. One of the services is to investigate cases, where both the petitioner (one who feels discriminated against) and the respondent (the party who allegedly has discriminated) are being heard. In spite of the so called reversal of the burden of proof, racial discrimination—because often subtle and part of an everyday process of accumulating incidents—remains difficult to 'prove' with legal instruments. Many Afro-descendants remain hesitant about using the services of anti-discrimination agencies such as the Equal Treatment Commission. They are skeptical about the outcome, or fear victimization, even when victimization is against the law.

Muslims

A not insubstantial number of people of Afro-descent in Europe are Muslims. Therefore racial discrimination cannot be seen as disconnected from old and renewed religious antagonisms between Christians and Muslims. In the same way, everyday (verbal) aggression against Muslims probably includes a mixture of racial, cultural and religious racism. In some countries, politically sanctioned anti-Islam campaigns (for instance against Moroccan-Dutch) are taking extreme forms. Freedom of expression is too often taken as the right to offend.

Negro

In the Netherlands, the term 'neger' (negro) is still commonly used to refer to dark skin people of African descent. Only recently, after years of protests, has the main Dutch dictionary included a qualification that some might take offense to the word as derogatory.

Opposition

In a number of countries opposition against racism is organized in cooperation with other communities of color and with (white) antiracist organizations, including those in the UK, the Netherlands, Germany, and France.

Political backlash has followed antiracism movements of the 1980s (UK, the Netherlands) and Sweden (late 1990s), often a result of changes in governments. In the new millennium there is growing Black (Afro) consciousness among young people, for instance, in the Netherlands, Germany and France. Urban Black Cultures are developing, often influenced by African American sports, arts and street cultures.

PATERNALISM

Afro- descent immigrants from the former colonies in the Caribbean are often exposed to racial paternalism: you can assimilate all you want, but you will never be seen as good enough (always as "not quite white/European") or as genuinely Dutch, French or British. The former colonized from the Caribbean are often not seen as a cultural threat because many are culturally integrated, which is also manifest in the presence of a substantial (highly educated) middle class. At the same time racial codes and barriers keep the highest levels of the labor market white. Exceptions are representatives in political parties and parliament.

QUOTAS

Occasionally, the quest for quotas is being suggested among activists as a remedy against social disadvantages and racial discrimination. Apart from the stigmatizing consequences, quotas do not solve the underlying problems of discrimination on the work floor, glass ceilings, racialized networking, or automatic preference for white candidates even when highly qualified Afro-descendants apply. Positive Action policies of the1980s (defined as: in case of equal competency between a White and a Black candidate, preference should be given to the Black candidate) seem to have reduced open discrimination in some cases, but did not lead to any preference for Black candidates.

RACE

Race is a legal category in European Law (antidiscrimination legislation). But race does not translate explicitly into policy making. For instance, race is not a formal policy category in Dutch political discourse. There is no formal registration on the basis of race, color or ethnicity. That does not mean that race is absent from cognitions and ideologies. In public discourse references to ethnicity, culture and religion (Islam) dominate; however, often notions of color are implicit.

SLAVERY

It is significant to notice that, in contrast to the US, slave plantation systems were established outside of Europe in the Caribbean and South American colonies.

In the US, knowledge about slavery and resistance has been transmitted from one African-American generation to another. This is not generally the case among Afro-descendants in Europe. Only recently former European slaveholding nations are acknowledging the wrongs of slavery (France) or integrating slavery into national histories (slave monument in the Netherlands).

Tolerance

Various Western European nations consider tolerance their national trait (for instance, the Netherlands and France). This is often mistaken for an absence of racism. Tolerance is a positive value in democratic societies; at the same time an overstated positive image blinds some to the reality of racial discrimination.

Unification

The unification of Europe has many political and economic purposes. But the racial dimension has not often been addressed. Unification can also be seen as the process of integration of white Europe. European identity builds (implicitly) on old racist theories of cultural hierarchies: from barbarian Moor to Muslim terrorist today; from black African cannibals at the height of colonialism to current media representations dominated by famine, corruption and warlords.

Dominant perceptions of Europeans are implicitly or explicitly 'white'. The idea that Europeans can be Muslim, brown or black should not be shunned any longer.

Violence

In Eastern Europe neo-Nazi and white pride physical violence against people of Afro-descent and other people of color is rampant.

Urgent policy interventions and international attention are needed to provide better protection for Afro-descendants in Eastern Europe.

Whiteness

Unlike the one-drop-rule in the US, biological determinism in Europe has not led to formal racial segregation. White is not a formal category and in most Western European countries explicit self-identification as 'white' is felt as something awkward because of the racial undertones. Ideologies of racial purity seem to have been less significant in some countries, including France and the Netherlands, where the emphasis has been more on cultural superiority. More research is needed, however, to make any definitive statements in this respect. It seems that systemic racial discrimination in Europe in the public sphere can go together with a high degree of racial mixing in the private sphere. This is an interesting area for research.

X-ing

Crossing racial borders through interracial relations is more common in Western Europe than in the US. The Netherlands is an interesting example, where substantial numbers (I believe 30% or more) of Caribbean immigrants of Afro-descent—in particular, the generations born in the Netherlands—have white Dutch partners. There is a long tradition of acceptance of racial mixtures, in particular among immigrants from the Caribbean former colonies (Suriname a case in point), where many before immigration already exhibited integrated racial backgrounds (African, European, Asian, native American). As a result, it is not taken for granted that people of mixed racial descent identify as 'Afro-' (only). It may well be that sections among Afro-descendants in the Netherlands follow the route of Indonesian immigrants, where next generations of racially mixed people gradually assimilate racially and culturally into the white dominant group. In this respect too there is a difference with the US.

In the UK and in other countries new generations are claiming recognition of their identity as 'mixed race'.

YOUNG PEOPLE

In the 1970s and 1980s much has been written about second generations being 'in between cultures'. New insights insist that 'in between' is not accurate in describing the experience of young people born in Europe, often of parents who were at least schooled in Europe. These are people who are living with, and easily switching between various cultural systems, across generations and across racial-ethnic borders, especially in the larger cosmopolitan cities. In the Netherlands, for instance, new languages occur among young people of all racial-ethnic backgrounds. High school Dutch—in particular, in the larger cities—is heavily influenced by Afro-Surinamese words and accents, occasional Berber words (Moroccans), overlaid with African-American rap codes, American-English expressions, and Anglo-sized Dutch words.

A notable number of young writers of Afro-descent are contributing to local and international literature in the UK, Germany, France, the Netherlands, Italy and possibly other countries as well. The same holds true for the performing arts and music.

ZWARTE PIET

Zwarte Piet is Dutch for Black Peter, the servant of Santa Claus. This Sambo looking figure, in fact a White person with blackened face, enlarged red lips, wooly wig and huge round earrings, is close to representing the Dutch national pet, or Santa Claus mascot. Dutch Santa Claus is celebrated on 6 December. In the month leading up to 6 December Zwarte Piet images can be found in schools, climbing ropes in shops, or jumping and dancing around in other public spaces. Many, but not all, people of Afro-descent experience exposure to these images as denigrating, offensive, if not racist. Some are called 'Zware Piet', at this time of the year by Dutch children. Attempts to ban this 'Blackened Peter' image have been met with fierce objections and emotional responses from white Dutch who feel this is their tradition, and nothing to do with racism.

PREPARED STATEMENT OF ALLISON BLAKELY, AUTHOR AND HISTORIAN, BOSTON UNIVERSITY

The history of Blacks in modern Europe is converging with the present situation that finds an unprecedented level of Blacks in Europe proper. The size and significance of this Black presence (see map) are not yet widely recognized by scholars or the general public. In fact, it has recently been overshadowed by manifestations there of the new clash between the West and Islam. While Blacks in Europe themselves are only beginning to sense a degree of group identity—and this largely forced upon them by the shared experience of discrimination and racism—the black population in Europe has finally achieved a size and visibility that invites comparison with the involuntary definition of community that shaped the concept of Afro-America among the descendants of enslaved Africans in North America.

For centuries millions of peoples of Black African descent were subjected to domination by the leading European societies in their colonies and former colonies abroad. In those settings there was a clearly understood hierarchy of wealth, power, and skin color; any Black presence in Europe was severely restricted; and European societies could pretend that those peoples were not part of their world. History is now converging with the present in that largely economic motivations are compelling the Europeans to allow into their midst populations earlier defined and treated as inferiors, and challenging what were supposed to be democratic societies offering equal opportunity to all for advancement.

As a result, in all of the societies that are most affected issues surrounding poverty and social exclusion are becoming apparent. The past few years have witnessed manifestations of the potential this fosters for social turmoil. One example from the eastern edge of Europe is the documentation of hundreds of incidents of violence against Blacks in Russia over the past decade, including several hundred murders. Especially troubling is that the only constructive governmental response there has been to silence the press through intimidation so that such incidents are no longer reported to the public at home or abroad.

Meanwhile, on Europe's western edge, the ethnically charged protests that spread to 300 cities in France in late October and early November, 2005 featuring deadly violence and thousands of burning automobiles, easily evoked scenes from the major urban riots in the United States in the 1960s, or in Europe, the disturbances in 1981 in London's Brixton district. These were followed a few months later by much larger disturbances in Liverpool's Toxteth district. The British government inquiry into the causes of the Brixton disturbance conducted by Lord Leslie Scarman in November of 1981 addressed underlying causes that were reminiscent of the 1968 Kerner Commisssion Report on conditions in the United States. The Kerner Commission Report attributed the American riots to the failures of American society to integrate African-American rural-to-urban migrants and their descendants, which were reflected by high unemployment, abusive police practices, substandard housing, inadequate education, poor recreation facilities and programs, and inadequate response from established institutions. Now, a few decades later, a survey of reports emerging from several European countries read like excerpts from the Kerner and Scarman inquiries. In the same vein, attorneys for the families of the two teenagers killed in the 2005 violence in France filed a complaint with the courts charging what amounted to racial profiling and police negligence strikingly reminiscent of perennial complaints of police misconduct all-too-familiar in the United States' inner-cities. While much of the world was more surprised to learn of France's clusters of suburban (banlieue) poor than it was of those abandoned in New Orleans during hurricane Katrina earlier in 2005, such ghetto-like settlements of ethnic and religious immigrants in Europe are not unique to France.

Racial thought and racist stereotypes are playing an especially prominent role in this scenario. For example, it is estimated that about 30% of the African ethnic and religious minorities involved in the disorders in France were black. Thus one major development to watch in the near future concerns the question of a Black identity in Europe. For example, is there taking shape a blanket "Black" identity that is applied to all people of predominantly Black African descent, regardless of their place of origin, and regardless of their own self-identification? For centuries peoples of Black African descent have struggled to escape the designation of "Black" originally imposed upon them in the course of European imperialism and colonialism.

They wanted instead to retain the identities of their respective native cultures, or to simply be accepted as full human beings with equal respect in whatever culture they found themselves. However, it is not clear whether even now in the twenty-first century this has become a reality. Despite the fact that a Black woman, Baroness Valerie Amos, originally from Guyana, has served as leader of the House of Lords in England, and Christiane Taubira from French Guiana drew some 2.3% of the vote in the 2002 Presidential election in France, star black soccer players in Europe still endure having bananas and racial epithets hurled at them on the field; and a study in England in late 2007 found that Blacks are 7 times more likely to be stopped by the police than whites.

The main reasons the image and status of Blacks continue to suffer seem to be economic. Just as the lure of profit from the slave trade, slavery, and maintaining a cheap labor force made it advantageous to define Black Africans into an artificial racial category, the profits from popular racial stereotypes in such areas as the advertising industry, entertainment, and sports have served to perpetuate color bias. The following questions merit much further research and discussion:

- Are old stereotypes of Blacks still relevant today?
- Are people of Black African descent in Europe considered Europeans, Africans, or simply Black?
- How do people of Black African descent in Europe self-identify?
- What is the most likely outcome of the identity of Blacks in Europe?

One encouraging sign that responsible elements in European societies are aware of the seriousness of this problem is that both national and European Union human rights organizations are forming as are civil rights and black consciousness groups. It is also worth noting here that some leaders in Europe are looking to the civil rights history of the United States for guidance. For instance, the largest black consciousness organization in France, the Conseil représentatif des associations Noires de France [Representative Council of Black Associations in France—CRAN] is consciously modeled after the NAACP, and a Black History Month is celebrated in more than a dozen European countries. These efforts deserve as much support as possible, in order to promote peaceful integration of the new, multicultural Europe.

PREPARED STATEMENT OF CLARENCE LUSANE, INTERNATIONAL RACE POLITICS AUTHOR, AMERICAN UNIVERSITY

Good morning. I want to thank the Committee for providing the opportunity to discuss what is emerging as one of the most important issues confronting the future of Europe: the status and means of social inclusion for people of African descent.

For more than 20 years I have worked with minority communities and NGOs, including people of African descent, in Europe focused on issues of human rights, immigration, racial equality, and intolerance. This work included several years as Assistant Director of the 1990 Trust, a black human rights organization based in the UK. In that and other capacities I also worked with governments and regional institutions, such as the European Union and the Council of Europe regarding these concerns.

Although the oldest skull ever found in Europe belonged to an African, and even African Americans have been living in England since the late 1800s, for most people in Europe a settled presence of black people is viewed as a relatively new phenomenon. In fact, there have been several waves of blacks to Europe since the end of World War II. In England, France, the Netherlands, and even Germany, black migration was critical to the rebuilding of Europe. Waves of blacks came to Western Europe to drive the buses, nurse the sick, and sweep the streets of its great cities. In Eastern Europe, communist states from Russia to Poland to Yugoslavia welcomed African students, scholars, artists, and other professionals as part of an effort to aid liberation movements and newly-independent states. These new populations merged with older small black communities.

However, in both Western and Eastern Europe, blacks and other minorities were never fully integrated into these societies. First, they have often been the target of violent, racist attacks. Skinhead and neo-fascist organizations in Russia, Austria, Germany, and other states have specifically targeted blacks and a number of individuals have been murdered in recent years.

Second, there remain persistent disparities in the social arena. In housing, education, health care, and other areas, blacks in Europe are at or near the bottom. In the UK, one of the few states where racial statistics are kept, black students are expelled at 2–3 times the rate of White Europeans, have an employment rate that is 18 percent lower than the general population (57%–75%), and are 50 percent more likely to die of a stroke.

Third, racial issues are also acute in the realm of criminal justice. Police violence, deaths in custody and disproportionate incarceration are major concerns in England, France, Spain, Germany, Italy, and a number of other states in the region. Again, in the UK, black people are six times more likely to be stopped and searched by the police, and three times more likely to be arrested than whites. In France, police-community tensions erupted into deadly riots in 2005. The racialization of crime and the criminalization of a race both are having a devastating impact on black communities in Europe.

Fourth, blacks are also suffering from the often harsh, unfair, and discriminatory immigration policies that exist in the region.

Anti-immigrant sentiments are rampant and not just restricted to the far-right, making it difficult to pass needed reforms.

RECOMMENDATIONS:

First, it is important that states begin to collect social and economic data on the situation of racial and ethnic minorities in the region. Understandably, the history of Nazism, fascism and ethnic cleansing has generated a reluctance to gather racial data, but the lack of empirical data continues to hamper the development of concrete policies that can effectively address the social exclusion of Europe minorities.

Second, there is a need to strengthen the content and enforcement of anti-discrimination laws and policies. The 2000 Race Directive from the EU provided a foundational framework for constructing polices that can address discrimination. However, the legislation only covers EU member states, and is focused on anti-racism. Legislation must begin to address the issue of racial equality and means by which progress can be made to close the disparities that currently exist and are growing.

Third, along these lines, it is critical to establish effective and empowered government agencies that are focused on anti-discrimination. These entities should be built in such as manner that they maintain independence from political parties and narrow government interests. The United Nations has outlined specific guidelines on the development of these types of government-related bodies.

Last and perhaps most urgent, there is a need to include the voices of black communities in the development of anti-discrimination and equality policies. A wide range of black and anti-racist NGOs have developed over recent years but have too often been excluded from the policy debates that are critical for the communities they seek to represent.

Thank you.

PREPARED STATEMENT SUBMITTED FOR THE RECORD BY BORIS KODJOE, ACTOR

Chairman Hasting, thank you very much for inviting me to participate in this very important and timely hearing. I am pleased that you are focusing on the experience of Afro-descendants in Europe, as this is a story that has received little attention and yet, is certainly a profound part of my own and the continents' history.

Growing up in a small town in Germany over thirty years ago, the situation was quite different than today. While my family and I may have been atypical for Germany at that time, we certainly did not feel unwanted. In this regard, my story may differ from others. There were no neo-Nazis parading through our town or far-right parties such as the National Democratic Party of Germany (NPD) brandishing anti-migrant posters or calling for persons who looked like me to be thrown out of the country. We were proud to be Black, German, and everything else that embodies being a Kodjoe. It was that foundation that was also critical to a small town boy becoming a world famous actor and owner of the global fashion company Ziami.

However, major events in world history such as September 11th have certainly in their wake also highlighted a more negative side to all of our societies. As a product of different cultures, and now the father of multi-cultural children—German and American, our emphasis must be on finding the similarities that unite, instead of divide us. This is the reason I have in the past been active in helping youth learn to embrace and benefit from cultural diversity and fight racism and ignorance. In this regard, I have also noted the efforts of the "Initiative Schwarze Deutsche" or the "Initiative of Black Germans." Having lived in Europe, Canada, and the US, the countries of the OSCE region have much to learn from one another. I see this hearing as a major opportunity to solidify transatlantic linkages and look forward to continuing to work with the Helsinki Commission in this fight.

Chairman Hastings, it is my understanding that you are preparing legislation related to this issue. Please consider me an early supporter of these efforts.

On behalf of my family and myself, thank you.

MATERIAL SUBMITTED FOR THE RECORD BY BRIMA CONTEH, DIASPORA AFRIQUE

Mr. Chairman
Distinguished Members of the Commision
Ladies and Gentlemen,

I wish, on behalf of my organisation—DIASPORA AFRIQUE to extend our sincere appreciation to this commission for holding this public hearing on the situation of people of African descent in Europe. I also take this opportunity to warmly thank our African-American members and sympathisers in the United States who facilitated and encouraged our participation in these hearings.

First of all I will focus my presentation on our organisation- DIASPORA AFRIQUE, and it's work in combating racism. This will be followed by a broad presentation of people of African descent in Europe: presence in Europe, movement patterns, issues, (integration), challenges and perspectives. Then I will look at anti-discrimination legislation with a particular focus on the EU race directive.

Mr. Chairman, our organisation was established to promote dynamic political, economic, social and cultural actions among people of African descent in Europe. We lay great emphasis on the past, present, and future interactions between Europe on one hand and Africa and it's diaspora on the other hand. The first concrete initiative to attain this objective was to map the African diaspora in Europe in it's contemporary political, economic, social and cultural dimensions, collect data and establish the required networks. After five years of tours of various cities in Europe, and bilateral discussions, the organisation has established contacts and networks in: Austria, Czech Republic, Belgium, France, Germany, Hungary, Italy, Ireland, Latvia, Luxemburg, the Netherlands, Poland, Portugal, Russia, Slovenia, Spain, Sweden, Switzerland, Russia, and the United Kingdom.

Consolidation of these networks and contacts is in progress. Local chapters have begun to be established in some countries; while the mapping exercise and data gathering for the rest of Europe is being pursued. We hope to embark on solid institution building to advocate for our rights and coordinate our political, economic, social and cultural activities in the not too distant future.

DIASPORA AFRIQUE has been active in Europe wide campaigns against racism and all forms of discrimination. We are members of the various national coordination of the European Network against racism (ENAR) and have been encouraging our networks and contacts to be part of the network. Today, there is much greater participation and visibility of people of African descent in this network .

Moreover we share information on best practices and reach out to communities of African and non-African descent. Our work on the EU race directive: holding regular consultations in the communities in France and sharing information have been of benefit to the entire community.

The growing number of hate crimes in parts of central and eastern Europe motivated us to intensify contacts with our brothers and sisters from these regions and link their struggles with those in the west. We have and still continue to encourage the participation of our brothers and sisters from Russia at the European Social

Forum to give them a wider audience where they can testify about the everyday racism they face in Russia because of the colour of their skin. We equally use this forum to move the EU race directive beyond the traditional anti-discrimination and Human rights network and engage greater civil society. We organised a roundtable on the EU race directive at the 2004 European Social Forum held in Paris.

DIASPORA AFRIQUE took part in the World Conference Against Racism in Durban and we have been actively participating in the deliberations of one of the mechanisms developed out of this conference: the UN working group on people of African descent.

I will now come to the second part of my presentation which is about our presence in Europe, movement patterns, challenges and perspectives.

AFRICAN PRESENCE IN EUROPE: Involuntary and Forced Migration

Mr. Chairman, various historical accounts attest to the presence of people of African descent in Europe way before the 1500's. We will however limit our presentation to population movements pertinent to this hearing.

THE TRANSATLANTIC SLAVE TRADE: BLACK CARGO TO EUROPE

(a) The UNESCO slave route project states that between 200–300,000 slaves were forcibly deported from Africa to Europe during the Transatlantic Slave Trade. Their presence, inferior and degrading status and roles in European society still play a role in the way people of African descent are perceived.

We can for this period quote famous names like Oladuah Equiano who played a leading role in the abolitionist movement in England and subsequent repatriation in 1787 of some of Britain's Black poor to Sierra Leone—my country of origin. Others in England include Emilio Sanchez based on our conversations with Steve Martin.

In France, Joseph Boulogne known as the 'chevalier de Saint Georges' born as a slave in Guadeloupe, came to France at the age of 7, and rose to become one of the earliest European classical musicians with African ancestry.

We had in the course of one of our "meet the brothers and sisters tours" mentioned earlier on; the opportunity to learn from Berlin based African-American Historian Paulette Reed-Andersen about German participation in the Transatlantic Slave trade as she took us on a historical tour of Berlin. 'Moorenstrasse' a Berlin street where enslaved Africans used to gather and which exists to this day in Berlin as tangible evidence of German participation and the African presence.

We hope through 'Black Cargo to Europe' a collaboration project between us and Dr. Paulette Reed Andersen's centre—to document, produce, and circulate educational material about this period of African presence in Europe.

HUMAN ZOOS—1860'S—1870'S

(b) Africans were paraded sometimes naked in various European cities during colonial exhibitions to give credence to and perpetuate the prevalent racist theories of the time as well as satisfy European public curiosity. 1998 French World cup champion Christian Karembu from French Caledonia, had his great grandfather exhibited in France. These exhibitions also called the 'Human Zoos' were at times organised by former European slave merchants.

BASTARDS OF THE RHINELAND

(c) Between 1920 and 1923, an active and intensive campaign was launched against French colonial African soldiers stationed in the Rhineland (Germany). French Historian Jean Yves Le Naour in his book 'La Honte Noire' says African soldiers were called "monkey men of the dark continent", "human animals", 'Black hyenas'.

What began as a local protest in the Rhineland became national at first, then European and international campaign against African soldiers, as the press across Europe joined the fray to fan the embers of hatred and racism on a daily basis. Bastards of the Rhineland was how Hitler referred to offsprings of relations between African Soldiers and German women. Bastards of the Rhineland were subsequently sterilised in a bid to cleanse and purify the German race.

Negritude launched by Aimé Césaire and Léopold Sédar Senghor during their student days in France in the early 1930's has to be seen as the Black man's attempt to reconquer his dignity as a human being against this background of heavily laden prejudice and animalisation of his essence. The intellectual production of these two giants projected in the French language to the world stage more than any other French intellectual in the last century.

Aimé Césaire joined his African ancestors on April 17th 2008. The French establishment lined up in his native born Martinique to pay their hommage, respect and consideration denied to him in his lifetime because of his uncompromising condemnation of racism and colonialism.

POST WORLD WAR 11 TO PRESENT DAY

(d) After World war II, people of African descent from the Caribbean were brought in to help rebuild devastated Europe. The United Kingdom for instance brought in Jamaicans and other English speaking Caribbeans. At the same time the number of students of African descent at European universities increased.

As of the 60's to the early 80's more people of African descent from sub-Saharan Africa came to Europe to work, study, and or stay facilitated partly by the legislation on Family reunion. Structural adjustment in the third world, dwindling resources, instability, in the 80's and 90's created conditions for more people to leave Africa and the Caribbean for Europe. We can posit from these movement patterns that the African presence in Europe from the Transatlantic slave trade to the present day has largely been involuntary and dictated by the needs of European societies. People of African descent like other migrants to Europe were later criminalised and their presence in Europe used as a launching pad into politics by extreme right wing forces.

RACISM AND ANTI-DISCRIMINATION LEGISLATION

The fact that we as a people have been reduced at some point in History to the status of animals means that a lot has to be done to elevate us to the status of normal human beings. Post World War II Europe having defeated Nazism with the participation and contribution of the formerly colonised had a moral obligation to combat racism and all forms of prejudice. With prejudice, racism and the supposedly inferior status of African people deeply steeped in the European psyche and without any serious attempts to deconstruct these myths, various models were proposed to create conditions for coexistence and harmony.

People of African descent were for instance firmly invited to 'integrate into European society'. This model prevailed in France and other European countries. The rising hate crimes in eastern and central Europe brought in the tolerance and intolerance models. The tolerance and intolerance models focus on individual acts and prejudice and not the collective and structural aspects of racism. Multiculturalism and Cultural diversity are the current models in fashion brought about not by public institutions but by the growing assertiveness and physical presence of 2nd, 3rd 4th etc. generation children. African-American Hip-Hop culture also plays a fundamental role in this regard.

With no serious policy programs to debunk the centuries old prejudice and myths about people of African descent, it is not surprising that we sometimes face the worst forms of discrimination in racial profiling, housing, employment, access to public and private services. Please allow us to repeat, there is to date no specific policy program in Europe aimed at combating the specific type of racism faced by people of African descent. Yet we are the elephant in the room.

We see stark evidence of the segregated status of people of African descent throughout our 'meet the brothers' and sisters tours. In 2004, about 50 men, women, and children of African descent were gutted by fire because they were living in some of the worst squalid and deplorable housing conditions inside Paris. This tragedy occurred barely two days after Katrina in New Orleans. DIASPORA AFRIQUE present on both sides of the Atlantic organised an event in Paris bringing together Katrina survivors and those of the Paris fires.

The plight of people of African descent is best expressed in the works of artists: singers, dancers, musicians, poets etc. throughout Europe in various languages. Celebrated UK dub poet Linton Kwesi Johnson for instance denounces police brutality in the United Kingdom in his 'License to Kill', and young Afro-portugueese rapper CHULAZ denounces the everyday racism in Portugal.

The first piece of antiracist legislation in Europe came about as a result of the Brixton race riots in 1976 in England. Elsewhere in the rest of Europe, racism was until the advent of the EU race directive not considered as issues worthy to bother legislators. As a result, some countries had some form of legislation while others did not. It was not until around 1999 that a treaty provisions addressing the question of racism and discrimination came into existence.

The 2000 EU race directive introduced the principle of equal treatment and laid down the basics for combating discrimination based on racial and ethnic origin. Provisions of this directive covered: access to education, health, employment training, goods and services, and housing. Member states are expected to transpose the directive into their respective national laws, consult with their respective civil societies, build institutions to combat racism and discrimination, and the burden of proof shifted from the victim to the aggressor.

The directive is the most advanced antiracist and antidiscrimination legislation in continental Europe. It is not unfortunately implemented as it should be because of a lack of political will. A number of Euro MP's sensing this lack of political will launched a campaign to name and shame countries which do not properly implement the directive. The European Network Against Racism(ENAR) in a July 28th press release expressed the organisation's extreme disappointment with the failure of 14 member states to properly transpose European race equality laws into their national laws.

We believe that the race directive properly implemented will increase confidence between law enforcers and citizens. In France this could have perhaps given more confidence to the two teenagers who ended up being electrocuted in 2005 because they were running from the police just as much as the police could have stopped running after the two teenagers. We all know that the tragic electrocution of these two teenagers was the trigger for the 2005 uprisings first in the Paris suburbs then the rest of France and even to one or two neighbouring European states.

CONCLUSION

We recognise the tremendous measures taken to combat racism and discrimination over the past two decades in Europe by both civil society and governments. We believe however that more has to be done to combat racism and discrimination generally.

We also recognise the efforts to focus on specific forms of racism and discrimination and we support and encourage the pursuit of such efforts.

We would like to invite European bodies in charge of combating racism and discrimination to equally focus on the specific form of racism against people of African descent. We would to end by making the following recommendations:

• Resources be allocated to organisations and individuals working on the specific issues of people of African descent

• Research institutions be set up or encouraged to develop studies on the interactions between Europeans and people of African descent

• A report on the specific form of racism against people of African descent be published in the literature of European antidiscrimination bodies such as the EUMC.

• Greater interaction between the EU antiracist bodies and the UN working group on people of African descent.

Finally, I would like to add that during the 2005 uprisings in France I was regularly interviewed by the BBC and other media groups like CNN. A BBC Journalist interviewing me for 'The World Today' programme asked if I thought the uprisings could spread to

other countries in Europe. In reply I said: As long as the deep root-
ed historical injustices which gave birth to the current socio-economic segregation are not properly addressed, then the uprisings
are bound to spread to other parts of Europe. Two days later incidents were reported in two neighbouring European countries.

MATERIAL SUBMITTED FOR THE RECORD BY INITIATIVE BLACK GERMANS (ISD)

HISTORY OF THE ISD

BLACK ORGANIZATION IN GERMANY—A HISTORIC DIGEST

In 2005, the New Black Movement* looks back to 20 years of its existence.

> 20 years of self-defining, of searching, of discovering and of excavating of buried roots in this country, 20 years of networking on the personal and the organizational levels, locally, regionally, nationwide and internationally.

The movement was started by Black Germans, people of African descent, who wanted—had to—break out of the isolation of a post-Nazi Germany and thereby were searching for autonomous definitions of their existence and for their own and appropriate concepts of life. The term "Black Germans", as well as the term "Afro-Germans" are self-definitions, which were coined in the beginning of the Black Movement which started to organize in the 80ies. They displaced all discriminatory denominations of the majority population that were effective to that date and since allowed for the denomination and evolution of a humane (self-)portrayal of black people in Germany.

Under the name of the ISD (Initiative Black Germans), local Initiatives blossomed in cities like Munich, Stuttgart, Freiburg, Hamburg, Hannover, in big parts of NRW and in the Rhine-Main region, which individually kept on working on the main idea and thereby little by little changed their life coherences and their perspectives and aspirations. Even before both of the German post-war countries were unified in 1989, black people on both sides of the "iron curtain had" contacted each other. Also in the then GDR, black people had organized themselves, e.g. in Berlin (east), Dresden or Leipzig. With time advancing, the Black Movement, which always acted and oriented itself locally and on the national level at the same time, grew. ISD and her sister organization ADEFRA (Afrogerman Women / Black Women in Germany) were always a driving force. ISD still remains committed to the idea of being an initiative, but also not to forget amidst the impetus of new efforts.

The New Black Movement changed its self-conception following internal discussions reviewing the first 20 years of its history by becoming incorporated and adopting the name 'ISD-Federal', which captured the nationwide activities taking place since the 90ies under the title of "Black People in Germany". This was conducted not to forget the history of self-definition and self-assertion, but to build on this foundation.

All branches of ISD have set themselves the task of creating opportunities for a self-determined dialogue of the African diaspora in Germany, to process black German history and generally make these issues as well as the general issues of the black people / people of African descent publicly heard and seen. In this sense, var-

---

*While processing our history, we found out that Africans had founded respective associations with the aim of assisting one another in coping with matters of everyday life and of forming a lobby for people of African descent in the colonies as well as in Germany since the beginning of the 20th century particularly in colonial metropolitan areas like Hamburg and Berlin.

ious publications came into existence such as Afrolook 1986–1999), Afrekete (published by ADEFRA during the 80s), Blite-youth magazine (published by ISD-Berlin, 1999–2002). Additionally, online forum like www.afronetz.de, www.afrolink.de, www.cybernomads.net, and www.isdonline.de emerged.

The tradition of an annual nationwide gathering organized by and for black people was also established, where discussions, knowledge exchanges, and opinions could be formed and the community of old and young in the African diaspora could simply be enjoyed. From these gatherings, the Sankofa meeting emerged, a self-organized meeting of black parents and their children, and— for the first time in 2004—a gathering of the "YoungStars", the black youth and hopefuls. Also legendary are the events of the Black History Month (BHM 1990–2001), which fostered a broad cooperation of African/black German groups. To the regret of many BHM tourists and Berlinians, the Black History Month slowly dozed off due to organizational reasons, but in 2004 the first Black Community Weeks once again began incorporating the respective experiences and successes of BHM. In the meantime, the ISD's approach stands in solidarity with the many African associations and individuals across the nation, who also put the circumstances of life in Germany on their agenda. During annual meetings of the Black Community, representatives of the Black German diaspora gather in order to produce common concepts for political and educational work and to build a common foundation, which is built on mutual acceptance and communication. The principles of ISD and Adefra have fostered a strong tradition of close-knit networks.

POLITICAL AREAS OF THE ISD

Black Germans, who survived the Nazi regime with its humiliations, disfranchisements and (illegal) sterilizations, had learned to attract as little attention as possible. Despite Article 3 of the German constitution, even after the Nazi regime, the racism which had been established since the days of colonial aspirations, latently still blossomed without bumping borders. In comparison to the USA (racial segregation/civil rights movement) and the African continent (colonialism until the 60ies and Apartheid in South Africa until 1989), the racist patterns of action in Germany were downplayed. Still, the so-called "latent" racism after 1945 meant, for approximately two generations of Black Germans, being deprived of their own voice, their own opinions and feelings, and professional and personal possibilities of development, in short, being squeezed to the edge of society.

The racist ideological reasoning why black people couldn't be Germans, was in the meanwhile replaced by an omission in written history. According to this omission, black people in Germany could not be Germans because they allegedly did not appear in German history. The acquisition of black German history became thereafter an essential instrument of emancipation. The initial lack of interest of the majority population enabled black Germans to develop a self-determined picture of black German history of their own on the empty field of their alleged non-history and position it against the established way of history writing. Thereby, writing history was analyzed as an instrument of authority on the basis of own experiences and discovered as a political area of action.

This process was accompanied by a confrontation about citizenship. Citizenship should in a democratically oriented society not be defined by "volkish" but rather by formal criteria. Such a latitudinal policy tenor would eschew the debates about the German citizenship, about naturalization and multiple citizenship, about immigration and the immigration society and put them on more solid premises. German identities would no longer be queried on the basis of a questionable canon but would be understood as the reflection of multi-"ethnic" equal ancestry.

The ISD contributes with its work to unmasking two basic lies of the German "majority-"society: "Racism does not exist in Germany" and "Germany is not an immigration society". With images of fear of "foreign infiltration", a modernized form of racism is being fueled concerning immigration and asylum policies. That in the meantime, immigration is also talked about as a fact is not a paradox. Because the debates are being carried out by different protagonists and progressive approaches disappear very quickly behind restrictive calculuses of "security policies". In everyday life, the face of "modern" racism displays itself when for example agents of the federal police hunt unwanted refugees at the Cologne central station. The pretended recognition by undifferentiated stigmatizing images is notorious. Regularly and first of all, such parameters strike black people, no matter which legal status regarding residence or citizenship they have. And this we must fight together.

ISD represents the interests of black people in Germany vis-à-vis the public and decision makers. For instance, ISD intervenes with public statements around debates of non-discrimination laws. ISD intervenes in cases of discrimination by supporting the victims and raising publicity. ISD qualifies internally and externally new anti-racists, and serves as afro-centrist multipliers in the areas of education and training and arranges expertise.

ELEONORE WIEDENROTH-COULIBALY (ISD–BUND) and SASCHA ZINFLOU (ISD–NRW)

MATERIAL SUBMITTED FOR THE RECORD BY BLACK EUROPEAN WOMEN CONGRESS

CELEBRATING BLACK EUROPEAN WOMEN

The existing wealth of documentation regarding the presence of African derived peoples in Europe points to the fact that Blacks have been and still constitute a growing segment of the European population. However, despite such documentation, the existence of these groups has been mainly ignored in the recording of European history (Earle and Lowe: 2005). Black women in particular have either been "invisible" or their bodies and persona pathologized within European historiography.

Organised within the framework of the "European Year for Equal Opportunities" and initiated by Beatrice Achaleke, AFRA (International Centre for Black Women's Perspectives in Vienna, Austria, and co-organised by Helen Felter, representative of Tiye International (The Netherlands); the Black European Women's Congress (26–29 September 2007) made history by challenging what Paul Gilroy (2004: 141) has called "the peculiar synonymy of the terms European and white", and also offering a gendered perspective on what it means to be a Black European.[1] One hundred and twenty Black European women delegates from sixteen European countries and the United States arrived in Vienna, Austria, for the three-day conference. This milestone event culminated in the formation of the Black European Women's Network. The conference provided a space and platform for the strategic discussion of various issues such as migration, political participation, qualification and access to the labour market, identity and self- empowerment, gendered racism, mechanisms of social exclusion, psychosocial conflicts (particularly women and children), and the role of Black European women within European societies.

The drafting of the Vienna Declaration (see: www.bewnet.eu), recommendations and strategic networking practices resulting from the conference will be used for lobbying on behalf of the needs and demands of Black European women on a national as well as European level.

An international symposium titled "The Future of Diversity Management in Europe" is scheduled for 12 March 2008 on the premises of the Austrian representative of the EU Parliament and Commission. The symposium will precede the follow-up strategic meeting scheduled 13–14 March 2008 in Vienna, Austria. For more detailed information regarding AFRA and the Black European Women's Network, please see both English language websites: www.blackwomencenter.org and www.bewnet.eu .

○

---

[1] The term Black European refers to individuals with ties to the African Diaspora, who were born and socialized within a European context.

This is an official publication of the
**Commission on Security and
Cooperation in Europe.**

This publication is intended to document
developments and trends in participating
States of the Organization for Security
and Cooperation in Europe (OSCE).

All Commission publications may be freely
reproduced, in any form, with appropriate
credit. The Commission encourages
the widest possible dissemination
of its publications.

★ ★ ★

http://www.csce.gov

The Commission's Web site provides
access to the latest press releases
and reports, as well as hearings and
briefings. Using the Commission's electronic
subscription service, readers are able
to receive press releases, articles,
and other materials by topic or countries
of particular interest.

Please subscribe today.

www.ingramcontent.com/pod-product-compliance
Lightning Source LLC
Chambersburg PA
CBHW080522290526
45790CB00006B/2275